"As one who teaches in the field of evangelism both in local congregations and in seminary—this is a book I have long been waiting for. I truly believe that Don's book has the capacity to unlock witnesses for Christ in this missional moment. We desperately need ways to set people free to tell the story of Christ. Filled with important statistical insight, amazing stories of witness, vulnerable examples, and rich biblical insight—this book is simply a must for the church today."

Jim Singleton, associate professor of pastoral leadership and evangelism, Gordon-Conwell Theological Seminary

"Don lets us walk in his shoes, beginning with shy Don who avoids spiritual conversations, to open Don who finds great joy in the simple conversations of life. In addition, the book is rooted in thoughtful statistics, helping us see how faith today is different from twenty-five years ago. Don's style is folksy, winsome, insightful, convicting, and even fun. Enjoy!"

Doug Schaupp, national director of evangelism, InterVarsity Christian Fellowship, coauthor of *I Once Was Lost* and *Breaking the Huddle*

"I have long admired the life, work, and writing of Don Everts (*I Once Was Lost*). *The Reluctant Witness* now adds to my admiration. I was moved by it. Why? Over my forty years of ministry, I have seen spiritual conversations go from cool or hip to something as awkward as kids at their first junior high dance to it now being assumed that spiritual conversations will automatically get mixed up in our coarse, even hateful, civil discourse. Don cuts through all this. Using easily digestible data, he shows us that we really don't have to be so guarded, so afraid, so on our heels. Don gently leads us toward renewed confidence as spiritual conversationalists. I can't think of a more timely and well-aimed book on evangelism."

Todd Hunter, Anglican bishop, former director of the Alpha Course USA, author of *Christianity Beyond Belief*

"The vast majority of Christians I know want to share their faith but find themselves hesitant for a variety of reasons. Don understands our concerns because he shares them; he too was a reluctant witness. Don masterfully weaves together his own journey and cutting-edge research with practical applications to help people take easy steps on the road to sharing their faith. If you, your small group, or your church want to share your faith but can't seem to take those steps in daily life, I plead with you to read this book!"

Dana S. Allin, synod executive of ECO: A Covenant Order of Evangelical Presbyterians, author of *Simple Discipleship: Grow Your Faith, Transform Your Community*

"*The Reluctant Witness* is the best book on evangelism I have read in years. It will convict you, inspire you, and train you at the same time."

John Ortberg, senior pastor of Menlo Church, author of *Eternity Is Now in Session*

"This is a delightfully helpful and practical book! Conversations about Jesus don't have to be a conflict-ridden, relationship-damaging affair. Don shows us to how to have faith conversations, and when we do, he offers research to show they not only bolster our faith but also make most involved— whether Christian or not—glad! Read this book and be encouraged to start a faith conversation. I know I am."

James Choung, author of *True Story* and *Real Life*

"Reminders are extremely important, and *The Reluctant Witness* delivers them. Don Everts draws us back to what we already know: sharing the gospel is about intentionality, keeping things simple, and stepping outside of our comfort zone and entering into conversations. Convicting! Challenging! Encouraging! Everts takes us by the hand and in a most gracious way, equips us for a world where we often neglect to go but must for the day approaches!"

J. D. Payne, associate professor of Christian ministry, Samford University, author of *Evangelism: A Biblical Response to Today's Questions*

Don Everts

The Reluctant Witness

Discovering
the Delight
of Spiritual
Conversations

IVP Books

An imprint of InterVarsity Press
Downers Grove, Illinois

380 8377

InterVarsity Press
P.O. Box 1400, Downers Grove, IL 60515-1426
ivpress.com
email@ivpress.com

InterVarsity Press® is the book-publishing division of InterVarsity Christian Fellowship/USA®, a movement of students and faculty active on campus at hundreds of universities, colleges, and schools of nursing in the United States of America, and a member movement of the International Fellowship of Evangelical Students. For information about local and regional activities, visit intervarsity.org.

Scripture quotations, unless otherwise noted, are from The Holy Bible, English Standard Version, copyright © 2001 by Crossway Bibles, a division of Good News Publishers. Used by permission. All rights reserved.

While any stories in this book are true, some names and identifying information may have been changed to protect the privacy of individuals.

All figures, unless otherwise noted, designed by Chaz Russo, data visualizations developed by Roxanne Stone, Barna Group; copyright Lutheran Hour Ministries.

Figure 4.8, "Big Story Diagram," is from James Choung, True Story *(Downers Grove, IL: InterVarsity Press, 2008). Used with permission.*

Figure 5.7, "Spiritual Conversation Curve," designed by Sarah Eischer, copyright Lutheran Hour Ministries.

Cover design: David Fassett
Interior design: Jeanna Wiggins
Images: abstract watercolor: © lutavia / iStock / Getty Images Plus

ISBN 978-0-8308-4567-5 (print)
ISBN 978-0-8308-6556-7 (digital)

Printed in the United States of America ♾

InterVarsity Press is committed to ecological stewardship and to the conservation of natural resources in all our operations. This book was printed using sustainably sourced paper.

Library of Congress Cataloging-in-Publication Data

Names: Everts, Don, 1971- author. | Barna Group.
Title: The reluctant witness : discovering the delight of spiritual
  conversations : featuring original research from Barna / Don Everts.
Description: Downers Grove : InterVarsity Press, 2019.
Identifiers: LCCN 2019007985 (print) | LCCN 2019012974 (ebook) | ISBN
  9780830865567 (eBook) | ISBN 9780830845675 (casebound-cloth : alk. paper)
Subjects: LCSH: Oral communication—Religious aspects—Christianity. |
  Conversation—Religious aspects—Christianity. | Witness bearing
  (Christianity)
Classification: LCC BV4597.53.C64 (ebook) | LCC BV4597.53.C64 E94 2019
  (print) | DDC 248/.5—dc23
LC record available at https://lccn.loc.gov/2019007985

P	19	18	17	16	15	14	13	12	11	10	9	8	7	6	5	4	3	2	1
Y	34	33	32	31	30	29	28	27	26	25	24	23	22	21	20	19			

Dedicated to

all the conversation partners
God has placed on my path—
past, present, and future.

Contents

Foreword

Roxanne Stone,
Editor in Chief, Barna Group

THE MESSAGE OF CHRISTIANITY has not always been wielded with grace. Many people know Christianity more for what it's against than what it is for. To be against something (or *someone)* is frowned upon in America today. *Tolerance* is the word of the day—and while tolerance is certainly a beneficial virtue in a pluralistic society where we must find a way to live alongside one another, walking the fine line between tolerance and one's convictions is a difficult challenge for many Christians.

Indeed in our research, we saw that a fear of giving offense or being rejected is one of the primary barriers for many Christians when it comes to talking about their faith. The number-one reason people told us they don't have more spiritual conversations is because "religious conversations always seem to create tension or arguments." Christians told us that when it comes to their faith in society today, they feel misunderstood (65%), persecuted (60%), marginalized (48%), silenced (46%), and afraid to speak up (47%). When nearly half of practicing Christians feel afraid to speak up about their faith, it is no wonder fewer and fewer are doing so.

Because you've picked up this book, I'm going to go ahead and assume you're actually interested in talking about God. But, perhaps like me, you've noticed that doing so has become more and more difficult. The words once shared by common belief seem almost foreign now—*grace, justice, charity, sin, forgiveness, holiness*—you can't speak them without needing to define them. (Which maybe isn't such a bad thing, really? Maybe being forced to give some real thought to these profound concepts is a worthy challenge.)

In the pages of this book, through Don's clear prose and compelling stories, I hope you'll find the encouragement and inspiration you need to wade into the tricky tides of spiritual conversations. And I pray the real-life data from Barna will help you recognize the issues making those conversations difficult, so you can engage with knowledge and respond with empathy.

The spiritual conversations I've had over the years have not always been fun—they haven't always led to spiritual awakening. But like the eager conversationalists you'll meet in this book, I came to find them rewarding and always, always worth the effort.

Let the conversation begin.

"Everyone who calls on the name of the Lord will be saved."

How then will they call on him in whom they have not believed? And how are they to believe in him of whom they have never heard? And how are they to hear without someone preaching? And how are they to preach unless they are sent? As it is written, "How beautiful are the feet of those who preach the good news."

ROMANS 10:13-15

Introduction

Are My Feet Beautiful?

SEVERAL YEARS AGO I was sitting in the window seat of a Greyhound bus heading from the desert town of Ontario, Oregon, to the rainy town of Tacoma, Washington. This 500-mile route normally takes about eight hours to drive, which translates to about a fifteen-hour bus ride. It turns out buses do unusual things like obeying the speed limit and stopping in *every single little town* on the way. Or so it seems.

In the seat next to me was a woman in her early thirties who, for 13½ hours, I didn't say a single word to or even acknowledge. For 13½ hours! There were several stops along the way (remember, *every single little town*) where one or both of us would get off the bus to buy food or use the facilities. Then we'd get back on the bus, sit in our a-little-bit-too-close-for-comfort seats on the left side of the bus, and continue to not talk.

Why the conspicuous lack of conversation? I suppose part of this is normal. Have you ever noticed there's a special set of social rules when we are on planes, trains, and buses—a sort of public transportation Cone of Noninteraction? When we are sitting next to someone on a crowded plane or bus or light rail, it is completely acceptable to not interact. Even though we are sitting uncomfortably close for long periods of time, even though our shoulders and elbows may actually touch from time to time, it is acceptable to not engage in any sort of conversation while in the Cone of Noninteraction.

But if I'm being honest, there was more than that going on during our silent bus ride. I may have been silent, but as the bus ride stretched on there was a sort of escalating war going on inside of me. You see as a Christian I know I am sent by Jesus to be a messenger of his to the people around me. I knew this that day as I sat on the bus too. In fact, I was an intern with Inter-Varsity Christian Fellowship, basically a campus pastor in training. So I knew clearly that Jesus was in the business of rescuing people and that I had been enlisted in that mission.

As a campus ministry intern I was quite familiar with Paul's simple logic in that Romans 10 passage at the beginning of this introduction:

Anyone who calls on the name of the Lord will be saved.

But how will they call on someone they don't believe in?

And how will they believe in someone they've never heard about?

And how will they hear unless someone tells them about him?

I knew all that. In fact (this is where the story gets a little embarrassing) for the first 13½ hours of the trip I was reading a book. It happened to be a book about—evangelism. Yes, I was enjoying Becky Manley Pippert's call to relational evangelism, *Out of the Saltshaker and into the World*, while completely ignoring the human being seated two inches from my right elbow and shoulder.[1]

And at first the irony was lost on me. (Did I mention this is an embarrassing story?) I had been asked to read the book by an older Christian, and so I was. I found it to be well-written and captivating, though I have to admit I felt there wasn't much new about the content. I already knew that followers of Jesus were called to witness to and share with others about Jesus. (I even taught this as a campus intern.) I was just, to put it simply, not planning on doing that. Ever.

To say I was a reluctant conversationalist would be an understatement. I was not interested in striking up even a pedestrian, everyday conversation with the woman seated next to me. To use Pippert's language, I knew I was "the salt of the earth," but I had little interest in leaving the saltshaker.

Why? I guess I felt I was called to the college campus and that "contact evangelism" (being open to spiritual conversations with people you've just met) just wasn't my thing. But also, I suppose, it really was a combination of apathy, shyness, and basic fear. And some simple logic: I assumed spiritual conversations were pesky, painful, awkward things, and I make it a habit to avoid pesky, painful, awkward things. Therefore, logically, 13½ hours of silence.

But this is where the war within me began to rage. You see, during that silence I was reading Becky Pippert's book. And while the call to witness in the book was not new to me, the *spirit* and *tone* of the book were. Becky wasn't laying on a guilt trip: *All Christians must engage in pesky, painful, awkward conversations. This is your duty.* On the contrary, Becky simply told story after story of everyday, surprising, even *delightful* conversations. She wasn't like a drill sergeant wagging her finger and insisting I dutifully engage in spiritual conversations. She was like a happy swimmer waving her hand and beckoning me to get off the dock and join her in the waters of witness: *Come on in, the water's great!*

And that sense of delight was, to me, new. Could spiritual conversations really be enjoyable? Pleasant? Delightful even? Turns out this is the surprising conclusion of Paul's logic in Romans 10, and the part of the passage I had never really paid much attention to:

And how will they hear unless someone tells them about him?

And how will they tell unless they are sent as witnesses?

As it is written, "How beautiful are the feet of those who share good news."

How beautiful are the feet? I don't know about you, but I have rarely heard of feet being referred to as "beautiful." Beautiful feet? What exactly is Paul saying? That people who share the news of Jesus have attractive feet? For that matter, what was Isaiah (whom Paul is quoting here) saying?

> How beautiful upon the mountains
>> are the feet of him who brings good news,
> who publishes peace, who brings good news of
>>> happiness,
>> who publishes salvation. (Isaiah 52:7)

Closer inspection reveals that Isaiah and Paul were proclaiming exactly what Becky was describing in her book: that there is something *beautiful* about sharing with others about God's salvation. It's not that their literal feet are pretty, it's that their mobility and readiness and willingness to talk are attractive and delightful. Talking about God with the people around you is, according to Isaiah and Paul, beautiful.

And thus the growing war within me on that bus. My allergy to conversations was grounded in the hard certainty that spiritual conversations were pesky, painful, awkward things. But there was Becky happily treading water next to Paul and Isaiah, and all three seemed to be waving their hands, smiles on their faces, beckoning me to quit the dock and jump in: *Come on in, the water's great!*

And so somewhere about three quarters into the book (13½ hours into the bus ride), the war within me came to a crescendo. *Are the waters of witness really great? Is it really beautiful to start walking up a mountain of a conversation in hopes that it may become a spiritual conversation? When Jesus told his disciples "You will be my witnesses" (Acts 1:8), might that have actually been a joyful invitation rather than a sober sentence?* I had to find out.

So after 13½ hours of riding in complete silence, I turned to the woman seated next to me and said (get ready for it):

"Hi."

Did I mention this story is a little embarrassing? Perhaps not the smoothest first step onto the trailhead of a conversation, but a step nonetheless. The woman seated next to me flinched just slightly, and her eyes widened. (What must she have been thinking to be greeted after so many hours of silence?) But she smiled politely and said:

"Hey."

And there we were, both of us, on the trailhead of a conversation. I would take a next step in the conversation. And so would she. And where the trail of that conversation eventually went floored me. Changed my life forever, and perhaps hers as well.

At the end of this book I'll tell you the whole fun story. But for now, I simply want to place before you the assertion that was memorably placed before me that day: *there is something delightful about spiritual conversations.*

Not only does God's Word proclaim this, but brand-new research conducted in partnership between Barna Group and Lutheran Hour Ministries confirms this as well.[2] And that's what this book is all about. It is my hope in the following pages to not only unpack what God's Word clearly states about the nature of spiritual conversations but to also take seriously what the latest research reveals (perhaps surprisingly) about people's experience of spiritual conversations. My conversation on that bus and many conversations since have convinced me that this is a vitally important endeavor.

You see, as it turns out, since that bus ride God has taken me on a path that has involved numerous spiritual conversations. Though I was once such a reluctant (perhaps even stubbornly reluctant) conversationalist, God has invited me to labor with InterVarsity Christian Fellowship on college campuses for eighteen years and to labor as a pastor for ten years. Those twenty-eight years have been utterly filled with spiritual conversations.

Along the way I've also become intimately involved with a popular spiritual conversation model and a spiritual conversation ministry that have both given me a bird's-eye view of thousands of additional spiritual conversations than I normally would have had access to. The net result? I find myself treading water right next to Becky and Paul and Isaiah. And this book is simply a biblically grounded, research-based way of waving my hands to Christians everywhere: *Come on in, the water's great!*

More to the point, the water is delightful. And Jesus' call to be his witnesses, it turns out, really is a joyful invitation, not a sober sentence. Witness really is beautiful. And inside that insight rests the hope of the world and of your neighborhood. Normal Christians like you and me are the "sent ones" Paul refers to in Romans 10. In the end, people won't hear about Isaiah's "good news of happiness" unless they hear it from you and me. We are Jesus' plan.

So where do we go from here? We begin with an honest, perhaps uncomfortable, self-evaluation of the state of our witness (chap. 1), followed by an important reckoning with one particular fear that is causing so many of us to avoid spiritual conversations (chap. 2). And this is where things get exciting, because in chapter three we'll find out what the most current research tells us about how Christians and non-Christians alike *experience* spiritual conversations. The net result: the data actually bursts five popular myths most of us have about spiritual conversations. (The water really is better than you might have guessed.) Finally, in the last two chapters we get to know a group of people researchers call "eager conversationalists"— folks who are having a blast in the waters of witness. What do these eager conversationalists have in common (chap. 4), and can we begin to practice for ourselves any of their conversational habits (chap. 5)?

If you are a reluctant conversationalist reading this book simply because an older Christian has asked you to—keep reading. You may find yourself as surprised as I was on that bus ride. If you are an eager conversationalist wishing your conversations were more fruitful—keep reading. You may gain important wisdom about how non-Christians experience spiritual conversations. And if you are a leader struggling to mobilize more people to engage in more spiritual conversations—keep reading. You may find that perhaps Paul knew exactly what he was doing when he finished his logical progression in Romans 10 by poetically celebrating the beauty of witness.

In the end, my prayer is that the Scripture and data and stories and insights found in this book will confront you with wonderful news: that spiritual conversations truly are delightful. That the feet of those who share the good news really are beautiful. On the whole, Jesus' church in our new postmodern age has grown silent. But I wonder, *What if we started talking again? What if we began turning to the people next to us and simply saying hi more often?*

If the last hour and a half of my bus ride was any indication, the results would be, in a word, delightful.

CHANGES IN SPIRITUAL CONVERSATIONS OVER 25 YEARS

TODAY, CHRISTIANS ARE LESS LIKELY TO...

● 1993   ● Today

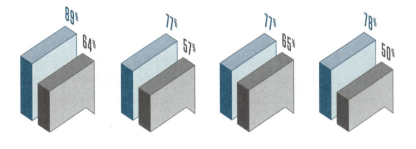

Believe every Christian has a responsibility to share their faith

Claim their church does a good job of training people to share their faith

Share by the way they live, rather than speaking about it

Speak about the changes/ benefits of accepting Jesus

FIGURE 1.1

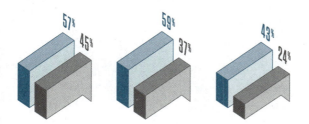

Tell the story of how they first came to believe in Jesus
57% 45%

Quote passages from the Bible when sharing their faith
59% 37%

Challenge someone to defend their beliefs
43% 24%

1993: *n*=446 Christians who have had a conversation about their faith, August 14–20, 1993;

Today: *n*=796 Christians who have had a conversation about their faith, June 22–July 13, 2017.

They devoted themselves to the apostles' teaching and the fellowship, to the breaking of bread and the prayers. And awe came upon every soul, and many wonders and signs were being done through the apostles. And all who believed were together and had all things in common. And they were selling their possessions and belongings and distributing the proceeds to all, as any had need. And day by day, attending the temple together and breaking bread in their homes, they received their food with glad and generous hearts, praising God and having favor with all the people. And the Lord added to their number day by day those who were being saved.

ACTS 2:42-47

1

Reluctant Conversationalists

Getting Honest About the State of Our Witness

I'M SITTING AT A GRAY METAL DESK in the basement of a nearly abandoned local church that has donated office space to some of us campus ministers. It's snowing outside the church, a beautiful Boulder, Colorado, winter day. But I'm not gazing out at the snow, I'm staring down at a blank sheet of paper that is confounding me.

This is odd. I'm a writer at heart, I like blank pages. I usually never meet a blank page I don't like—they inspire me and help me think. But I'm having a problem with this particular blank page. I work on a nearby campus for InterVarsity and I'm supposed to be writing my monthly report. My supervisor has asked me to look back at the last month and characterize my efforts on campus and assess the fruit that has resulted. Sounds simple enough. But I'm grousing. I'm confounded. I don't like this assignment.

Characterize my efforts on campus? How can you sum up in mere words and sentences thirty long days of labor that have been so messy, so sublime, so context-driven? And assess the fruit? How do you count spiritual fruit? Is it possible to quantify the fruit of relational evangelism? Is it even right to try to count spiritual fruit that only God can produce?

These were the lofty thoughts and justifications rolling around in my head as I stared at that blank sheet of paper. But mostly I was just insecure.

It is a tender thing to characterize your own efforts to share the gospel. All Christians are sent on a mission: Again, as Jesus said, "You will be my witnesses" (Acts 1:8). A witness talks about what they've seen or experienced. In this case, Christians are called to talk about their experience with Jesus so that others may have a chance to meet and ultimately follow Jesus.

Many of us know this. But to reflect on and characterize our faithfulness in that mission can be tender. Vulnerable even. It's enough to get your justification juices flowing, just like mine were while sitting at that metal desk staring at that blank sheet of paper.

This is especially true if you dare take the second step of evaluation I had been asked to take: to assess the fruit of my efforts. *Have I been a witness?* is a scary enough question to ask (though there's still plenty of wiggle room in that question). But to ask, *Have I made any new disciples?* That is an entirely different level of scary. It is vulnerable. And uncomfortable.

And for this reason, it is, I'm assuming, mighty tempting to lay this book (and topic) aside at this point. What good could come of getting honest about the state of my witness? A renewed sense of guilt? A burst of inspiration that sets me up to be disappointed once again? If these thoughts are going through your mind, I urge you to keep reading. I invite you to dare to get honest about the state of your witness for this reason: honest self-reflection about mission has been an explicitly important feature in the lives of Christians from the very beginning.

The Importance of Honest Self-Evaluation

The Acts 2 passage that you read at the beginning of this chapter is pretty well-known. It's exciting and inspirational. Luke (who wrote the book of Acts) gives a summary of the church's efforts and the resulting fruit that has motivated many generations of Christians as a beautiful snapshot of Jesus' church doing what that church was meant to do.

But it is also meaningful to pull back and notice the simple fact that Luke summarized a snapshot of the church. Luke did what was so difficult for me to do sitting at my desk: he characterized the church's efforts (they devoted themselves to . . .) and he quantified the fruit that resulted (and the Lord added to their number day by day). And here's something that should get our attention: he kept doing this, over and over.

Scholars have noted this important literary feature in Acts: regular snapshots of the church's efforts and the resulting fruit. In fact, many scholars suggest these 30,000-foot snapshots mark the basic structure of Luke's writing: a few on-the-ground detailed stories of God's work through the church punctuated by snapshots that characterize the church's mission and the resulting fruit.

These snapshots do two things: they characterize the church's labors (notice the verbs), and they also assess the resulting fruit (while the fruit of the kingdom of God is not always numeric in nature, here in Acts Luke does place an emphasis on the numeric). See table 1.1 for a few examples.

Luke didn't balk at providing a snapshot of the church's labors and resulting fruit, rather he leaned into it as if this were an important thing to do. And this should get our attention. If it was so important for the early church to regularly take a look in the mirror and have an updated snapshot of the "state of the church's mission," perhaps this is a habit we shouldn't set aside too quickly.

It can be painful to honestly evaluate our own witness. But it might turn out to be vitally important. I got a taste of that back in Colorado. Rather than give in to my insecurities and loftily justify my way out of writing an honest monthly report, I dared

CHARACTERIZE THE CHURCH'S LABORS	ASSESS THE RESULTING FRUIT
…they were *speaking* to the people… (4:1)	But *many* of those who had heard the word believed, and *the number* of the men came to about *five thousand*. (4:4)
Now many *signs* and *wonders* were regularly done among the people by the hands of the apostles. (5:12)	And more than ever believers were *added* to the Lord, *multitudes* of both men and women. (5:14)
And every day, in the temple and from house to house, they did not cease *teaching and preaching* that the Christ is Jesus. (5:42)	…the disciples were *increasing in number*,…and the *number* of the disciples *multiplied greatly* in Jerusalem, and a *great many* of the priests became obedient to the faith. (6:1,7)
So the church throughout all Judea and Galilee and Samaria had peace and *was being built up.* (9:31a)	And walking in the fear of the Lord and in the comfort of the Holy Spirit, it *multiplied*. (9:31b)
And Paul and Barnabas *spoke out boldly*… (13:46a)	And the word of the Lord was *spreading* throughout the whole region. (13:49)
As they went on their way through the cities, they *delivered* to them for observance the decisions that had been reached… (16:4a)	So the churches were strengthened in the faith, and they *increased in numbers daily*. (16:5)

TABLE 1.1

to look into the mirror. I characterized my efforts at sharing the gospel. (How often was I engaging in conversations with the people around me? Was Jesus ever coming up in those conversations? Was I spending any time with non-Christians, or had I filled up my life with Christian students?) And I even tried to assess the fruit that had resulted from my efforts. (How many non-Christians were involved in our group's events? Had anyone begun to trust Jesus for the first time?)

Writing that monthly report was awkward, but over time, month by month, I began to gain an appreciation for the model Luke left us. There is something right and healthy and refreshing about regularly taking a look in the witness mirror.

The State of Our Witness

How would you characterize your own witness efforts? A characterization must be accurate enough to truly name reality, but short enough to be memorable and useable. Getting to a place where you can honestly characterize your own witness efforts should take some time and work. The process should force you to reflect and think. We read one of Luke's characterizations of the witness of the early church at the beginning of this chapter: *they were devoted followers of Jesus and they had favor with all the people.* And the result? *God was adding to their number daily.*

So, how would you characterize your own witness? This is a tricky thing to do. It can be difficult to get perspective on ourselves, and Luke certainly isn't around to help us. So, let's begin this way: let's look in the mirror together. A big collective gaze in the mirror: How is the church in the United States doing with witness? This collective gaze should help us each jump-start our own personal self-reflection.

And this collective gaze really is possible because of a recent partnership between two Christian organizations. Lutheran Hour Ministries recently partnered with Barna Group to assess the state of witness in the US church. Their careful qualitative and quantitative research produced a fascinating snapshot of the state of witness in the United States.[1]

Comparing their findings with a similar study they did twenty-five years ago, Lutheran Hour Ministries and Barna Group have given the US church a gift: an accurate look in the mirror. Details of their findings can be found in the Barna Report *Spiritual Conversations in the Digital Age: How Christians' Approach to Sharing Their Faith Has Changed in 25 Years.*[2] But even a brief overview of what they found (as you can see in figure 1.1 at the beginning of this chapter) can help each of us kick-start our own self-reflection. So, what does this research show us about ourselves?

Finding 1. We are having fewer spiritual conversations. To put it simply, Americans today are less involved in spiritual conversations than we were twenty-five years ago. A "spiritual conversation" is defined as *any* conversation about spiritual or faith matters (including doubts) with *anyone.* This would include talking about Jesus with a non-Christian friend but would also include talking about the sermon you just heard with your spouse.

These spiritual conversations could have been in person but also could have occurred on the phone, via text, or even on social media. In this way the researchers used a fairly broad definition for spiritual conversations.

Yet even with a broad definition for spiritual conversations, as you can see in figure 1.2, most of us (74% of us) are having fewer than ten spiritual conversations a year. We are what the researchers characterize as "reluctant conversationalists."

As you look at figure 1.2, where do you intuitively think you land—on the reluctant or eager side of things?

How many spiritual conversations did you have over the last twelve months? (Spend time estimating and calculating this for yourself. How often do you talk with others about your faith?)

Finding 2. We are uncomfortable with spiritual conversations. On the whole our engagement in spiritual conversations has gotten worse over the last twenty-five years, especially when it comes to spiritual conversations with non-Christians. The reality is fewer of us feel adequately prepared to share about our

NUMBER OF CONVERSATIONS ABOUT FAITH IN THE PAST YEAR

% AMONG U.S. SELF-IDENTIFIED CHRISTIANS

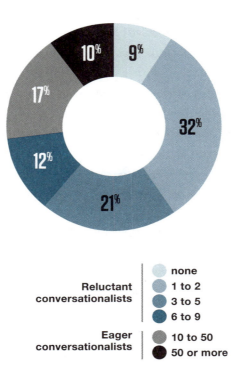

=796 U.S. self-identified Christians, June 22–July 13, 2017.

FIGURE 1.2

Christian faith. Only 57 percent of us feel our church does a good job of training us to share our faith—compared to 77 percent of us twenty-five years ago. If fewer of us feel equipped to talk about our faith, it makes sense that we are talking about our faith less.

Our level of discomfort isn't helped by the fact that more of us than ever will avoid talking about our faith if we feel our non-Christian conversation partner would reject us. Almost half of us (44%) are going to avoid spiritual conversations if we feel we might be rejected. That's up from only 33 percent of us twenty-five years ago. We are simply less comfortable having spiritual conversations with non-Christians.

How equipped do you feel to talk about your Christian faith (on a scale of 1-10)?

What does your church do to equip people to talk about the faith? How successful would you say that equipping is (on a scale of 1-10)?

How willing are you personally to start a conversation if you feel your conversation partner might reject you?

Finding 3. Our spiritual conversations mention Jesus and the Bible less. We are less comfortable talking with non-Christians about our faith, and when we do engage in spiritual conversations with non-Christians, what we talk about today is different. We are less likely to talk about the benefits of trusting Jesus: only half of us (50%) bring up how good it is to follow Jesus when talking with non-Christians (78% of us were bringing that up twenty-five years ago). We are less likely to tell the story of how we ourselves began to trust Jesus (45% of us, down from 57%). We are also less likely to quote from the Bible (37% of us, down from 59%), and very few of us challenge others to defend their own beliefs (24%, down from 43%).

As you can see in figure 1.3, we also pray less before talking with non-Christians about our faith, and we are more likely to use the same basic approach and content no matter who it is we are talking with. Given the diminishment of some of these basic Christian points of content, we might surmise that as Christians we have become more committed to sharing our faith through our Christlike actions rather than relying as much on verbal witness. But our look in the mirror actually reveals otherwise. It turns out that fewer of us seek to share Jesus through our actions (65%) than our counterparts twenty-five years ago (77%).

As you reflect back on the spiritual conversations you have had with non-Christians in the last year, describe what those conversations were like.

How comfortable are you talking about Jesus and your own life with Jesus? How comfortable are you talking about God's Word?

When conversations get around to Christianity do you have a "stump speech" that you tend to use every time, or are you more responsive and flexible based on who you are talking to?

THEN & NOW: CONTENT AND APPROACHES FOR SHARING FAITH

% AMONG CHRISTIANS WHO HAVE HAD A CONVERSATION ABOUT THEIR FAITH

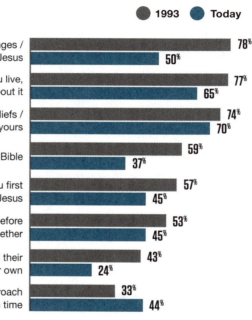

● 1993   ● Today

Speak about the changes / benefits of accepting Jesus — 78% / 50%

Share by the way you live, rather than speaking about it — 77% / 65%

Ask questions about their beliefs / experiences, tell them yours — 74% / 70%

Quote passages from the Bible — 59% / 37%

Tell the story of how you first came to believe in Jesus — 57% / 45%

Pray for the person before you get together — 53% / 45%

Challenge them to defend their beliefs, in view of your own — 43% / 24%

Use same basic approach and content each time — 33% / 44%

1993: *n*=446 Christians who have had a conversation about their faith, August 14-20, 1993;
Today: *n*=796 Christians who have had a conversation about their faith, June 22–July 13, 2017.

FIGURE 1.3

Finding 4. Our approach to spiritual conversations mirrors our surrounding culture. In their research project, Lutheran Hour Ministries and Barna Group didn't just take a look at Christians' approach to spiritual conversations, they also did a survey of the general population. What they found was that we Christians are not so different from our surrounding culture.

The research revealed that only 8 percent of Americans talk about God, faith, religion, or spirituality even once a week. Only an additional 15 percent talk about spiritual matters even once a month. The average American says they only have about one spiritual conversation a year. Americans are talking about spiritual matters less, and the American church seems to be following suit.

THEN & NOW:
CHURCH ATTENDANCE AMONG CHRISTIANS

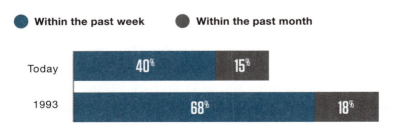

● Within the past week   ● Within the past month

Today   40%   15%

1993   68%   18%

FIGURE 1.4

Or rather, American *Christians* seem to be following suit. The reality is fewer and fewer Christians are actually an active part of a local church. In 1993 if you were a Christian the odds were you had attended a local church within the last week or last month (86% of us). But as you can see on figure 1.4, today it's just about a coin flip. Only 55 percent of Christians attended a local church in the last week or last month. That's only half of us. Perhaps it should not be surprising then that we Christians are not so distinct from our surrounding culture.

> **Where would you be on figure 1.4? How often are you getting together for church with other Christians?**
>
> **If you were to characterize your distinctness on a scale of 1 (I am exactly like the surrounding culture) to 10 (I am nothing like my surrounding culture), what would your number be? What do you think might be an ideal target number?**

Finding 5. We know spiritual conversations need to be initiated. The research has revealed that we are more convinced than ever that spiritual conversations with non-Christians don't just happen on their own. They take effort. Twenty-five years ago, most of us (75%) believed that opportunities to share our faith happened unexpectedly. Today only 61 percent think so. Perhaps this is why the number of

THEN & NOW: OPPORTUNITIES TO SHARE FAITH

% AMONG CHRISTIANS WHO HAVE HAD A CONVERSATION ABOUT THEIR FAITH

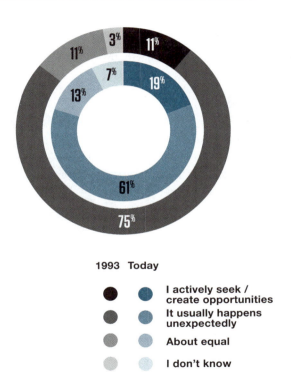

1993 Today

- I actively seek / create opportunities
- It usually happens unexpectedly
- About equal
- I don't know

1993: n=446 Christians who have had a conversation about their faith, August 14-20, 1993;
Today: n=796 Christians who have had a conversation about their faith, June 22- July 13, 2017.

FIGURE 1.5

us who actively seek opportunities to share our faith in a conversation has actually gone up slightly since 1993, as you can see on figure 1.5.

We also are more convinced than ever that genuine relationships (which take time and effort to initiate and nurture) are a prerequisite to effectively sharing our faith—47 percent of us, up from only 37 percent in 1993.

Taken together these numbers seem to suggest we are crystal clear that it takes effort on our part to help spiritual conversations occur.

> **Do you believe you need to build a genuine relationship before talking about your faith? Why or why not?**
>
> **Describe the role you believe you have in initiating such relationships and conversations.**

Finding 6. Our conversations increasingly have a digital element. You might be encouraged to know people are still experiencing big life changes because of spiritual conversations. This is what the research tells us. It also tells us that increasingly parts of those life-altering spiritual conversations are happening digitally: through email, text, social media, and so on. As you can see on figure 1.6, one's generation clearly plays a role in how likely it is that parts of your spiritual conversation happen digitally.[3]

INTERACTIONS THAT LED TO MY BIG LIFE CHANGE

% AMONG U.S. ADULTS WHO EXPERIENCED A BIG CHANGE AFTER A SPIRITUAL CONVERSATION; RESPONDENTS COULD SELECT ALL THAT APPLY

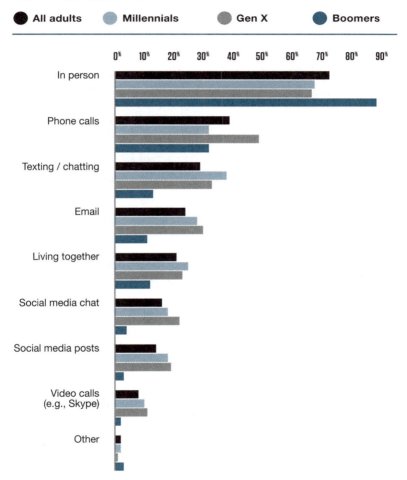

n=374 U.S. adults who report a big change after a spiritual conversation, June 22–July 13, 2017.

FIGURE 1.6

It's not surprising then that we are beginning to see the digital landscape as a valid and perhaps important place to engage in and initiate spiritual conversations. While having a spiritual conversation "in person" is still by far our most common way of proceeding (see fig. 1.7), we are beginning to use digital means as well.

In some sense, the verdict is still out on the effects this new digital element of spiritual conversations is having. Some of us (58% of millennials, 64% of Gen Xers, and 39% of boomers) believe sharing our faith has become *easier* because of our new digital landscape. But many of us (64% of millennials, 60% of Gen Xers, and 45% of boomers) have sensed people are more likely to avoid real spiritual conversations because they are so busy with their devices.

Scholars who study our digital behavior note we tend to curate our appearances more on social media (less vulnerability) and have a tendency to be meaner on the digital landscape ("online disinhibition effect" is the technical term), two tendencies counter to fruitful witness.[4]

So, we're a bit conflicted on *how* the digital landscape is affecting witness, but it is undeniable that conversations in general (and spiritual conversations in specific) increasingly have some digital element. These specific findings have led Lutheran Hour Ministries to embark on new initiatives that

HOW I HAVE SHARED FAITH VIEWS *AND* HOW OTHERS HAVE SHARED FAITH VIEWS WITH ME

% AMONG U.S. ADULTS WHO HAVE HAD A CONVERSATION ABOUT THEIR FAITH

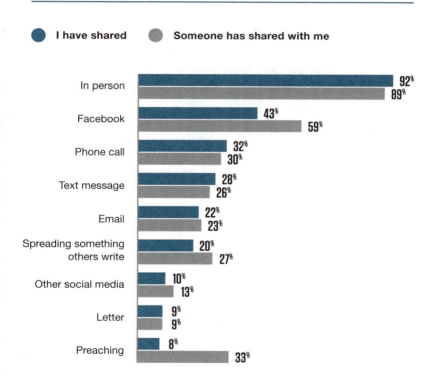

● I have shared   ● Someone has shared with me

	I have shared	Someone has shared with me
In person	92%	89%
Facebook	43%	59%
Phone call	32%	30%
Text message	28%	26%
Email	22%	23%
Spreading something others write	20%	27%
Other social media	10%	13%
Letter	9%	9%
Preaching	8%	33%

I have shared" n=840 U.S. adults, "someone else has shared" n=675 U.S. adults, June 22 - July 13, 2017.

FIGURE 1.7

engage the digital mission field, including equipping Christians to explore and commit to some core biblical principles for digital witness.[5]

> What generation do you fall into? How do you tend to view and relate to our new digital landscape?
>
> What percentage of your relationships would you say has some digital communication involved in it? Do you think that percentage is changing over time? If so, how?
>
> What experiences do you have sharing your faith digitally or seeing others do the same?
>
> What do you think are the biggest opportunities in this new digital age? The biggest temptations?

Assessing the Fruits of Our Witness

Hopefully, this gaze into the mirror has helped you begin to honestly evaluate your own witness. Of the six findings that the latest research has revealed about our collective witness efforts, which would you say is most helpful in beginning to characterize your own personal witness? Rate each of these on a scale from 1 (doesn't describe me at all) to 10 (that's me):

- I have few spiritual conversations.
- I am uncomfortable with spiritual conversations.

- My spiritual conversations seldom mention Jesus or the Bible explicitly.

- I approach spiritual conversations more or less like my surrounding culture.

- I know spiritual conversations need to be initiated.

- My conversations increasingly have a digital element.

Given what these reflections have revealed, how would you characterize your own witness efforts? Barna's research characterizes most Christians in the United States as *reluctant conversationalists*. Luke characterized the Christians in Jerusalem as *devoted, active witnesses*. These are characterizations. If you had to characterize your own witness efforts in just one phrase or sentence, what would it be?

This may be a painful thing to do—in fact, you may find that question to be as confounding as I found that blank piece of paper sitting at that gray metal desk back in Colorado. That question may make all sorts of defensive justifications spring up within you. But answering that question is an important step. Remember, it is possible something delightful may exist on the other side of that question.

Luke didn't merely characterize the state of the church's witness; he was also careful to assess and even quantify the resulting fruits. So, what fruit comes from your witness?

In this regard, the research we've been looking at can't help too much. The study was more focused on Christian activities (like the verbs from Luke's snapshots in Acts) than quantifying the fruits (like Luke's numeric observations in Acts).

But even a cursory view of the church in the United States shows we are not, on the whole, in a season of multiplication. We do have beautiful but rare occurrences of *multiplication*. We are also experiencing wonderful *addition* in some parts of the church. But on the whole, we're experiencing steady *subtraction*. How about you? What type of fruit have you seen as a result of your witness faithfulness? That winter day back in Colorado I had to admit I wasn't seeing much fruit.

These are, of course, very difficult questions. The questions become theologically tricky (doesn't God bring the fruit, not us?) as well as technically tricky (how exactly do you count making a disciple?), but this trickiness did not stop Luke from closely examining what was going on, and it should not stop us either. It is true that God brings the fruit, but he has called us to labor in his field, and how can we do that if we don't closely examine that field and even our own work habits as we prepare to enter the field? In fact, as Doug Schaupp, Val Gordon, and I explored in *Breaking the Huddle: How Your Community Can Grow Its Witness*, this honest self-evaluation turns out to be a key first step in allowing God to grow you in your witness.

It really is possible to experience the delight of spiritual conversations. It really is possible to have beautiful feet. But the first step is getting honest about your status quo.

IT'S UNACCEPTABLE TO SHARE YOUR VIEWS ON RELIGION...

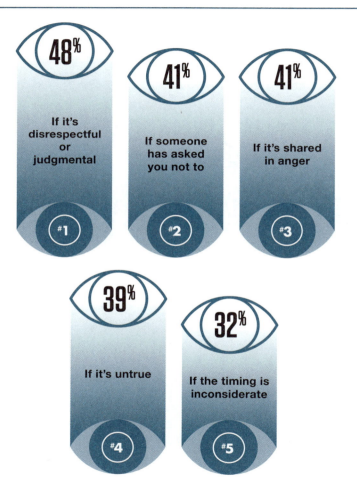

48%
If it's disrespectful or judgmental
#1

41%
If someone has asked you not to
#2

41%
If it's shared in anger
#3

39%
If it's untrue
#4

32%
If the timing is inconsiderate
#5

FIGURE 2.1

6 / 10 CHRISTIAN MILLENNIALS SAY PEOPLE ARE MORE LIKELY NOW THAN IN THE PAST TO SEE THEM AS OFFENSIVE IF THEY SHARE THEIR FAITH

(TWICE AS LIKELY AS CHRISTIAN BOOMERS)

% AMONG SELF-IDENTIFIED CHRISTIANS WHO HAVE TALKED ABOUT FAITH IN PAST FIVE YEARS

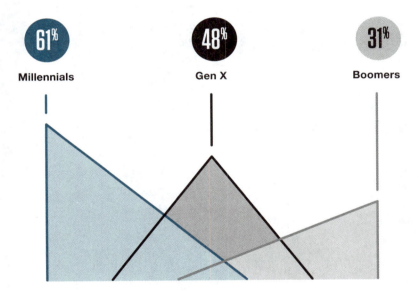

61% Millennials

48% Gen X

31% Boomers

n=1,070 U.S. adults, June 22–July 13, 2017.

FIGURE 2.2

They seized [Jesus] and led him away, bringing him into the high priest's house, and Peter was following at a distance. And when they had kindled a fire in the middle of the courtyard and sat down together, Peter sat down among them. Then a servant girl, seeing him as he sat in the light and looking closely at him, said, "This man also was with him." But he denied it, saying, "Woman, I do not know him." And a little later someone else saw him and said, "You also are one of them." But Peter said, "Man, I am not." And after an interval of about an hour still another insisted, saying, "Certainly this man also was with him, for he too is a Galilean." But Peter said, "Man, I do not know what you are talking about." And immediately, while he was still speaking, the rooster crowed. And the Lord turned and looked at Peter. And Peter remembered the saying of the Lord, how he had said to him, "Before the rooster crows today, you will deny me three times." And he went out and wept bitterly.

LUKE 22:54-62

2

Why We Stopped Talking

Meeting the Postmodern Cat That's Got Our Tongues

So, I'm listening to my colleague who sits one desk to the left of mine at a large company in the inner city of Tacoma, Washington. She's holding court, gesturing with her hands as she talks with me—witty as always—and I am smiling and nodding.

I am smiling and nodding, but I am not happy. And I definitely don't agree with a word of what she's saying.

Charlotte is smart and interesting and a great conversationalist. She's a reader and likes talking about what she's read. She recently finished a PhD and has a bright mind and, I have learned, a very sharp tongue. She's acerbic at times. There are times she politely gets off the phone with a client and then proceeds to absolutely fillet the person she just got off the phone with. Partly she does this for my benefit and entertainment, I think, and partly because that's just who she is.

I love talking with Charlotte; it makes the day go faster in between our calls on behalf of the company. Until, that is, the day she brings up Jesus. Charlotte is not a Christian, you see, and this is not a Christian company we are working for. In fact, I may be one of the only Christians working at our office. At the time I was a student leader in a Christian ministry at my nearby college campus. I was leading Bible studies, learning how to mentor younger Christians. I was even beginning to preach at our worship gatherings. I was getting used to talking with others about Jesus.

But it was different when Charlotte brought up Jesus and Christianity. Charlotte's tongue was so sharp and her words so educated-sounding as she mocked Christians and Christianity. And I just smiled and nodded. And then she said something that shocked me. "Of course," she said, her words coming fast and confident, "I don't think Jesus even ever existed. The whole thing is a myth."

I figured I had misheard her. I asked, "You mean you don't think Jesus was more than a man?" "No," Charlotte responded without missing a beat, "Jesus never even existed. There was never a man named Jesus, the whole story was made up years later by people looking for control." And then she went on to say lots of fancy, intelligent-sounding things. And I smiled. And nodded.

I wasn't happy. And I didn't agree. But I kept smiling and nodding. And I said nothing.

The Silencing Effect of Fear

There is a phrase in English many of us know: *the cat's got your tongue*. It's an interesting phrase and there's some fascinating debate about where it comes from. Some etymologists say the phrase hearkens back to the English Navy's use of a whip (called a cat-o'-nine-tails) they used for flogging people. The pain was such that when the whip had been used on someone, they stayed quiet for a few days. The cat got their tongue. Other etymologists bring us back to ancient Egypt where, for a time, those who were convicted of lies or blasphemy would have their tongues cut out and fed to cats. "Why doesn't that guy over there ever talk? Well, the cat's got his tongue." Other etymologists say the phrase has its roots in medieval fears of witches and their minion cats.

Regardless of what pain is being referenced, the phrase itself captures that universal phenomenon when fear keeps us from talking. Back in Tacoma, the cat had my tongue. Specifically, I was afraid of the social repercussions (aka Charlotte's derision) that would come if I were to defend Jesus or make it known that I not only believed he existed as a man but was also much more than a man.

This experience isn't unique to me, however. Many a Christian has remained silent because they feared what might happen if they brought up Jesus. In our culture there are times when speaking about our faith is pretty much the conversational equivalent of passing gas. Loudly. It can be awkward, embarrassing, and make people think less of us. Or cause people to make fun of us, depending on the crowd.

> Think about a time when you held your tongue about your faith for fear of social repercussions. How often would you say that happens?
>
> What is your primary fear at such times? What's the worst-case scenario you imagine in your head?

This is, in essence, the same thing that happened to Peter in that fireside scene in the epigraph (Luke 22:54-62) at the beginning of this chapter. Seems an innocent enough scene: a few townspeople sitting around a fire together, warming their hands. But there is a context—Jesus had just been arrested. So, for Peter there is real risk in being associated with Jesus, whether being made fun of or, worse, being arrested and punished alongside Jesus. To be associated with Jesus was risky for Peter. He was afraid of the consequences.

His fear was so strong that he actually denied knowing Jesus three separate times. The cat definitely had Peter's tongue. Fear is like that: it can control us, it can grab our tongues and keep us from talking. Back in Tacoma even as I sat smiling and nodding, saying nothing to Charlotte, I knew there was something unnatural about my silence. Something wrong, even.

I knew Jesus had called me to be his witness. And yet I said nothing. Even though I rationalized in my mind that there are times when speaking is not the best thing (something that's actually true), I nonetheless had a sense that being silent *because of fear alone* wasn't great.

Peter, I think, had the same sense. When the cock crowed and shook Peter out of his fearful posture, he realized what he had done. And wept. Being silenced by fear is not right and Peter knew it. After all, hadn't Jesus said once "Whoever is ashamed of me and of my words, of him will the Son of Man be ashamed when he comes in his glory and the glory of the Father and of the holy angels" (Luke 9:26)? And isn't there something admirable and attractive about Paul's brave pronouncement in Romans: "I am not ashamed of the gospel" (Romans 1:16)?

And yet the truth is, there are times when fear silences us. And that is not good. For the average Christian these days there are some big and gnarly postmodern cats that have got our tongues. Rather than remain silent, perhaps the time has come for us average Christians to look these fearful cats squarely in the eyes and confront them head-on.

The Postmodern Cat Named "Fear of Offense"

As Peter warmed his hands around that fire, he intuitively sensed he was sitting in a less-than-friendly context. (Jesus had just been arrested; the controversy over Jesus had hit the city like a wildfire; Peter had just cut off someone's ear, and that person was likely there near the fire! Peter was behind enemy lines.) There was some specific fear in his context that "got his tongue."

For about three hundred years after that night around the fire, most Christians lived in a similar less-than-friendly context. In fact, many Christians lived under the threat of some form of social, physical, or economic persecution until the Roman emperor Constantine converted to Christianity and officially decriminalized Christianity in AD 312.

Our context as Christians has varied widely since then. There have been seasons when great social coin came with being a Christian and speaking about Jesus (think John Calvin's Geneva in the 1500s), and there have been tough seasons of persecution (think genocides in the Ottoman Empire in the 1900s). This roller-coaster ride is perhaps what Paul was alluding to in his coaching words to the young leader and preacher Timothy when he invited him to "preach the word; be ready in season and out of season" (2 Timothy 4:2).

So how about us? Are you and I living when Christianity is "in season" or "out of season"? There are Christians in the world today who have enemies trying to do them harm because of their Christian faith. The persecuted church is a real thing. In some parts of the world being identified as a Christian can be a matter of life or death. In those parts of the world, Christianity is definitely "out of season." But if we're honest, most Christians in the West are not in that situation. We are not persecuted because of our Christian faith.

However, we are definitely experiencing less cultural privilege than we have for some time. For a few hundred years in the West, Christianity held a place of relative cultural privilege. In fact, during the modern era in the West, being a Christian made a person fit in, in a way. America was founded, in large part, by Christians, and Christianity has been mainstream in our country—until recently.

Many people mark the beginning of a shift in our culture in the early 1900s when we shifted out of the so-called modern era into something different. In the modern era Christianity was relatively "in season" in the West. But in our new era, referred to as *postmodern*, Christianity is "out of season" more and more each year. Christianity's cultural privilege is waning. And that doesn't feel good.

Just as Peter intuitively sensed the unfriendly context around him, so Christians today intuitively sense the same, as figure 2.1 shows. Even though Christians are still in the majority in the West and are not actively persecuted, according to Barna's research most Western Christians *feel* misunderstood and persecuted, and many of us also feel marginalized, silenced, and afraid to speak up.[1] As Barna and LHM's report puts it, the reality is Christianity is increasingly "out of season," and this trend shows no signs of slowing down. Our culture is increasingly secular (less and less colored by our Christian heritage) and more and more relativistic (looking down on exclusive truth claims). In this postmodern context the idea of attempting to convert someone else to your own faith is seen as religiously extreme by most Americans.

Even just sharing your views on religion has become less acceptable socially. As you can see in figure 2.3 we Christians are more open to sharing our views on religion than non-Christians, but even so only a quarter of us feel it's always acceptable to talk about religion. Turns out non-Christians are more comfortable sharing their views about other personal topics (like sexuality and health) than they are about religion.

And when it comes to sharing about your own religion, the world around us has a much broader sense of what conditions make discussing religion unacceptable, as figure 2.4 illustrates. While practicing Christians have a narrower view of what makes talking about faith unacceptable (indicated by a much smaller area on fig. 2.4), non-Christians have a much broader view of when it's unacceptable to talk about spiritual matters (indicated by the larger area on fig. 2.4). Today, talking about religion is being seen by more and more people as off-limits.

SHARING VIEWS ON THREE TOPICS

% AMONG U.S. ADULTS

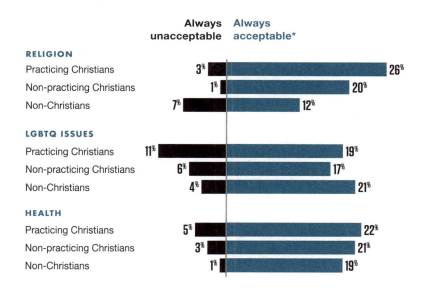

Always unacceptable   **Always acceptable***

RELIGION
Practicing Christians — 3% / 26%
Non-practicing Christians — 1% / 20%
Non-Christians — 7% / 12%

LGBTQ ISSUES
Practicing Christians — 11% / 19%
Non-practicing Christians — 6% / 17%
Non-Christians — 4% / 21%

HEALTH
Practicing Christians — 5% / 22%
Non-practicing Christians — 3% / 21%
Non-Christians — 1% / 19%

*"Never unacceptable" was the option in the survey; it has been changed here for clarity.
n=1,070 U.S. adults, June 22–July 13, 2017.

FIGURE 2.3

WHEN SHARING VIEWS ON RELIGION IS UNACCEPTABLE

% AMONG U.S. ADULTS

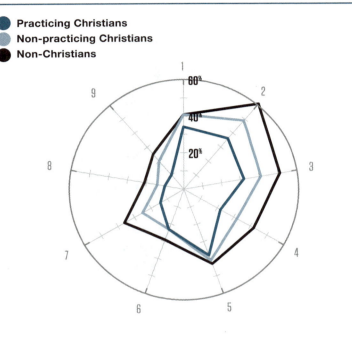

● Practicing Christians
● Non-practicing Christians
● Non-Christians

1. If it is untrue

2. If it is disrespectful or judgmental

3. If someone has asked you not to

4. If the timing is inconsiderate

5. If shared in anger

6. If it causes someone else to react in a bad way

7. If beliefs are shared as if they applied to everyone

8. If the other person can't respond

9. If discussed during work hours

n=1,070 U.S. adults, June 22–July 13, 2017.

FIGURE 2.4

One of the results of these cultural changes is that one of our ordinary fears has grown to large and frightening proportions. If a postmodern cat has got our tongues as Christians, this is that cat: the fear of offense. Or rather, *The Fear of Offense!* That's how it feels these days; this fear is ominous. We are afraid of offending others with our beliefs.

There has always been offense in the gospel. The good news (Jesus died to save us from our sins) always has bad news embedded within it (by the way, we are sinners). But that offense, on our postmodern landscape, is an unbelievably rude and vile social transgression. This fear of offense makes us believe talking about Jesus or the faith isn't just socially awkward (accidentally passing gas in a quiet room) but offensive and rude and aggressive. (I struggle with an analogy here: perhaps going up to someone and purposefully passing gas on them?)

Let's be clear; I'm not trying to be crass. I'm trying to adequately illustrate what the research tells us (and what we Christians intuitively sense)—that the fear of offense is incredibly strong these days. Our hesitance to talk about spiritual matters may have a number of causes (fewer relationships with non-Christians; not feeling equipped to talk about our faith) but one major cause in our specific context is this fear of offense.

If this fear is the postmodern cat that's got our tongues, then this cat is large and purple and mangy looking with sharp claws and protruding teeth! And make no mistake about it, this cat has got our tongues.

> **Think about your social circles; how off-limits is talking about faith?**
>
> **Describe a time when you personally didn't bring up your faith for fear of offending someone.**
>
> **Have you ever offended someone else by bringing up your faith? If so, what was it like? How did the conversation end?**

The Mechanics of Silence

In chapter one we looked at how much less we Christians are talking about our faith these days. The fear of offense has a silencing effect on us, and this is a serious situation: we're called to be witnesses and to not be ashamed of the gospel. And yet we are having fewer spiritual conversations. This is not good.

But the research reveals the seriousness of this situation. Not only are we Christians remaining silent, but we are also beginning to bend what we believe about our call to be witnesses of Jesus.

Consider what the latest research says about what we believe about evangelism. Twenty-five years ago, nearly every one of us who had had a spiritual conversation about our faith believed we had a responsibility to share our faith ("you will be my witnesses" and all that), as figure 2.5 illustrates.

THEN & NOW: WHAT CHRISTIANS BELIEVE ABOUT EVANGELISM

% AMONG CHRISTIANS WHO HAVE HAD A CONVERSATION ABOUT THEIR FAITH

● Agree   ● Don't know / neutral   ● Disagree

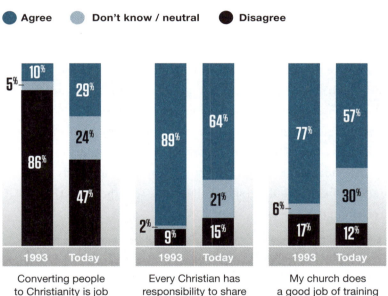

Converting people to Christianity is job of the local church

Every Christian has responsibility to share their faith

My church does a good job of training people to share faith

1993: *n*=446 Christians who have had a conversation about their faith, August 14–20, 1993;
Today: *n*=796 Christians who have had a conversation about their faith, June 22–July 13, 2017.

FIGURE 2.5

But today? Only 64 percent of us would say the same thing. In fact, twenty-five years ago most of us disagreed that converting people to Christianity was the job of the local church—we knew it was *our* job as Christians. Now only half of us disagree. In other words, what we believe about sharing our faith has changed.

As the fear of offense has grown, it would appear we have begun to shirk the responsibility to share about Jesus and our faith. We are not only growing more silent, we are also justifying that silence. More of us are viewing the task of bringing up Jesus as a task that belongs only to the professionals in the local church. This view of evangelism has the handy side effect of keeping us personally far away from the scary risk of offending anyone.

> Do you believe sharing the gospel is the job of the local church, or do you believe that responsibility lies personally with Christians? Or is it a mix?
>
> Have your views about evangelism shifted over time?
> If so, in what ways?

Peter's fear made him lie about Jesus, saying, "I do not know the man." Similarly, it would seem the postmodern fear of offense is making us lie to ourselves about our call to witness: "It's not my job to talk about the man."

Breaking the Silence

Rather than deny we are growing more silent as Christians, rather than grow hopeless because of how tempted we are to conform to our postmodern culture, it is refreshing and helpful for us to name what is happening, mourn it, and repent.

Isn't this exactly what happened with Peter? Peter was caught up in the weeds of his fears, parrying the questions of those around the fire who were sure they'd seen him with Jesus. Fear had his tongue—so much so that he resorted to outright lying about whether or not he knew Jesus. His fears had him.

But then something happened. A cock crowed. The sound jarred Peter out of his fearful trance and reminded him of the big picture. Jesus had prophesied Peter would deny him and, what do you know, that's exactly what happened. The harsh, jolting sound of the morning crow pulled Peter up out of the weeds of his fears and he realized what was going on. And then he did the most natural thing: he wept.

Peter didn't try to deny his actions, he didn't try to justify his lies. He faced it squarely and mourned how he had allowed fear to get his tongue. He mourned his silence. And this ultimately led to his repentance. Consider how remarkable it is that Peter not only became a fearless witness for Jesus, but he wrote letters to persecuted Christians encouraging them, too, to always be ready to talk about Jesus.

We should learn from Peter. The latest research is like a mirror held up to our own faces: it helps us see ourselves more clearly. And if we see fear and conformity, that can be a shocking realization, as shocking as a cock crowing. If that's the case with you, don't run from that reality. Face it squarely and mourn it. And repent. There is actually great hope for us as witnesses if we follow Peter's example.

> **How have the Bible passages and research findings in this chapter left you feeling?**
>
> **What are some of your own fears about spiritual conversations?**

There are other reasons for hope here in our postmodern landscape as well. The younger brothers and sisters among us (millennials and Gen Xers) are actually a bit more likely to view sharing Jesus as a responsibility of every Christian and to feel that responsibility personally. Could it be that those among us who are more native to this postmodern soil just aren't as surprised (and freaked out by) the fear of offense?

Where boomers and elders (who are more native to a modern culture) recoil at the growing fear of offense in our culture, perhaps our younger siblings are less reactive because they've lived with this fear of offense their whole lives. They are more used to this scary purple cat. We can all learn from them, especially millennials, because among them relational evangelism is actually on the rise.

There are some other data points that give us more reasons for hope too. Consider how many factors that affect our witness are ones we can actually control:

- Many of us who don't share our faith don't feel equipped to do so. (This is hopeful because we can actually get equipped.)

- More Christians today believe it takes a relationship with someone to have the context to share the faith. (This is hopeful because we can nurture genuine relationships.)

- It would seem unorthodox views of evangelism are contributing to our silence. (This is hopeful because we actually have the Bible to help us "be renewed" rather than "be conformed.")

- Once Peter faced his fears and repented of his silence, he became a quite fruitful witness for Jesus. (This is hopeful because it shows us that even someone who forsook his witness responsibility was welcomed back, embraced by Jesus, and able to get his tongue back.)

Peter's case study is such an interesting one. It's not that Peter had fewer reasons to fear going forward after that night at the fire. On the contrary, he had a whole litter of scary purple cats to confront. The difference was, after repenting, those fears didn't have his tongue anymore.

Peter and John (another early Christian leader) were once dragged before an intimidating council in Jerusalem. There was a whole lineup of intimidating, threatening cats in front of them: Annas the high priest, Caiaphas and John and Alexander and all who were of the high priestly family. Peter and John were dragged in front of them, threatened, and told to stop talking about Jesus. Peter's response? It's instructive and hopeful: "They called them and charged them not to speak or teach at all in the name of Jesus. But Peter and John answered them, 'Whether it is right in the sight of God to listen to you rather than to God, you must judge, for we cannot but speak of what we have seen and heard'" (Acts 4:18-20).

Peter still had fears to face; they just didn't have his tongue anymore. And the same is possible for each one of us. We too can pull our heads up from the weeds of our fears and face our fearfulness head-on. We can mourn our silence. We can name and confess the ways we've accommodated our culture and conformed to it, shirking our God-given call to be involved in delightful witness.

Can we control whether Christianity is "in season" or "out of season" during our life? Nope. But can we allow God's Spirit to empower us to live faithfully even though the gospel is out of season? Indeed. We can choose to listen to God rather than our fears.

And here's some wonderful news we got in our most recent research: Based on our intimidating fear of offense you might guess that spiritual conversations these days are tortured, awkward, painful things. Turns out reality is quite different than you might guess. According to the research, we don't have as much to be afraid of as we thought.

THERE ARE TWO SIDES TO EVERY CONVERSATION

DURING A SPIRITUAL CONVERSATION, PEOPLE REPORTED FEELING OR EXPERIENCING THE FOLLOWING:

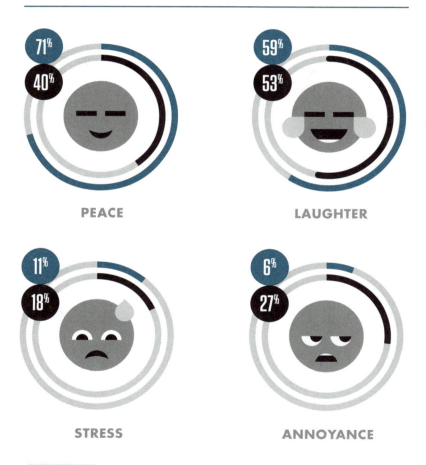

71%
40%

PEACE

59%
53%

LAUGHTER

11%
18%

STRESS

6%
27%

ANNOYANCE

FIGURE 3.1

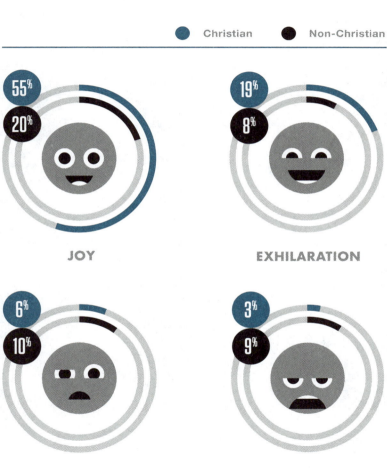

Christian

Non-Christian

55%

20%

JOY

19%

8%

EXHILARATION

6%

10%

CONFUSION

3%

9%

ANGER

How beautiful upon the mountains
 are the feet of him who brings good news,
who publishes peace, who brings
  good news of happiness,
 who publishes salvation,
 who says to Zion, "Your God reigns."
The voice of your watchmen—
  they lift up their voice;
 together they sing for joy;
for eye to eye they see
 the return of the Lord to Zion.
Break forth together into singing,
 you waste places of Jerusalem,
for the Lord has comforted his people;
 he has redeemed Jerusalem.
The Lord has bared his holy arm
 before the eyes of all the nations,
and all the ends of the earth shall see
 the salvation of our God.

ISAIAH 52:7-10

3

Delightful Conversations

Debunking Five Myths About Spiritual Conversations

IT'S WELL PAST MIDNIGHT and a late-spring Colorado snowfall is softly falling earthward, a few flakes landing on my glasses and blurring my vision as I look back at Rose. Rose is standing in the open doorway to her condo, and I am standing in the parking lot between her condo and my own. It's dark out and cold, but I don't mind. "Sweet dreams," she says.

Sweet dreams, I think. *God, what are you doing here?* I ask as I reflect on the conversation Rose and I had just had in her condo.

I had come over to Rose's condo around 11 p.m. as I often did to pick up a VHS tape. You see, I was a huge Denver Nuggets basketball fan, but my wife and I didn't have the cable channels we needed in order to get their games. Rose was a retired school teacher, a chain-smoking, cussing, vibrant woman in her seventies who had the most robust cable package money could buy. And so we struck a deal five years earlier when I moved in next door. I would do little fix-up jobs for Rose around her condo, and she would record each Denver Nuggets game on a VHS tape for me. (This was before DVRs were invented.)

One bonus part of this arrangement was that when I went over to pick up my VHS tape, we often would sit and chat, unhurried. We became friends in this way, even though the two of us were pretty different from each other. Rose was retired and dealing with the kinds of issues elderly folks deal with. I was working and dealing with the kinds of issues thirty-somethings deal with. Rose was an agnostic who dabbled in Native American spirituality, subscribed to theories of reincarnation, and had a bad taste in her mouth for all things Christian. I was a Christian missionary working on the nearby college campus. And yet we struck up a friendship.

In fact, our regular diet of unhurried conversations strengthened our friendship deeply over time. I would even say Rose became my best friend in Boulder. In ways, she became a part of my family—getting to know my wife, Wendy, and our kids, and spending holidays in our condo with us. Eventually, Wendy would send over a portion of every dinner she cooked to supply Rose with healthy food.

I never would have guessed Rose and I would become friends. The first time we ever met face-to-face was our first week in the condo when Rose knocked on my door to upbraid me for how I had put my recycling in the wrong containers in our shared trash room. She marched me over to show me how to correctly sort my recycling. During that first conversation, she made some off-handed mention of "church people" in a tone that made it perfectly clear to me that she had a distaste for all things Christian.

To be honest I was scared of Rose at first. She had a sharp mind and even sharper tongue, and given her allergy against Christians and all things having to do with Christianity, I assumed my usual posture in such situations:

I avoided her.

But then the Nuggets arrangement presented itself. And the next thing I knew, Rose and I were in regular unhurried conversations with each other.

And here's the thing: I enjoyed it. Even for an introvert like me there is something pleasant and right and *human* about being in conversation with another person. And the more we got to know each other, the more natural it was to fill Rose in on everything in my life: including my life with God. Within the warm light of friendship, it is the most natural thing in the world to share about our life with God. It was one of these spiritual conversations that led to our "sweet dreams" exchange in the parking lot that snowy spring night.

Earlier that night I was sitting in Rose's living room chatting with her when she asked how my week had been. Now, the reality was I had had a pretty intense week. I had a dream earlier in the week that woke me in the middle of the night. It was a vivid dream, so vivid I couldn't seem to shake it even after waking up the next morning. As a result, I spent much of my spare time during the week in prayer. It turned out to be an unexpectedly rich week of prayer. So, when Rose asked about my week, I wasn't planning on having a spiritual conversation or sharing the gospel with Rose, but the story of the dream and the time spent in prayer with God sort of came out as I shared about my week.

I almost didn't realize what was happening until the story was out in the room between us and Rose became fascinated by the dream and by my experience of prayer. Just like that, without me even really noticing it, we were having a spiritual conversation, and I was sharing with her about the God I followed and his Holy Spirit who now resided within me, and what it was like to be in an honest season of prayerful conversation with my God. Our conversation was alive, interesting, honest, provocative— and enjoyable. It was such a captivating conversation that time sort of got away from us.

Eventually, I realized how late it was, got my VHS tape from Rose, and we walked to her door. As I stepped out into the parking lot that was beginning to dust over with snow, Rose thanked me for sharing with her and then said, with a wink, "Sweet dreams."

And that's when my heart started to beat faster. Embedded in Rose's comment was a sweet blessing: *May your dreams trigger another week rich in prayer.* And the reality that everyday events can trigger our hunger for God settled over me with the spring snow. *Could an everyday event, like a dream, trigger Rose's hunger for God too? Could God use even this conversation we just had to trigger prayer in Rose's life?* The reality was as startling as it was obvious. And I waved to Rose standing in her doorway and said, almost as a benediction, "Sweet dreams to you too." *God, would you speak to Rose tonight? Could you do that? Could you use this moment our conversation has created to move in her life?*

I could barely sleep that night thinking about this conversation that had happened so naturally. I lay in bed praying, asking God to use that conversation and be moving in Rose's life.

And the next morning I woke up and wondered: *What's happening to me?* Don the introvert, Don the reluctant witness initiating and actually *enjoying* a spiritual conversation! What is the world coming to?

Upon reflection I realized what was happening to me was as natural and beautiful and unhurried as that late-spring snow making its way earthward: spiritual conversations are actually delightful things, rewarding things. There is something outright beautiful about talking with others about our God and what he is up to.

How Beautiful upon the Mountains

This is exactly what Paul made clear in that passage from Romans we looked at: "How beautiful are the feet of those who preach the good news" (Romans 10:15). And exactly what the prophet Isaiah made clear hundreds of years earlier in that beautiful passage in this chapter's epigraph.

Isaiah is prophesying about God's coming salvation. *God is going to come and save the day.* And given this rock-hard, undeniable truth of history, how beautiful it is when people bring the good news of that salvation. The act of announcing this news of salvation is not just good, not just right, not just important. It is *beautiful*.

What, exactly, is beautiful? The *feet* of those who bring good news—their willingness and mobility and activity in sharing the good news. In one of his letters Paul talks about putting on readiness "as shoes for your feet" (Ephesians 6:15), further playing on the metaphor of feet representing our readiness to share the good news. It is beautiful to share the good news.

Consider the parallel phrases Isaiah 52 uses to illustrate how delightful sharing the news of salvation is:

- publish peace
- bring good news of happiness
- publish salvation

There is something delightful about sharing the good news. And there's something imminent about sharing the good news: it brings the reality of God's presence and *aliveness* to light within the room. Isaiah puts it this way: "The LORD has bared his holy arm before the eyes of all the nations." God is active and present wherever his salvation is announced.

That's what got my heart beating in the parking lot that night. God's holy arm (his activity in the world) was present. Not only could God call me into prayer through a simple dream, but he could also call my neighbor into prayer through a simple conversation. God could show Rose his presence. And that realization was electric. My "Sweet dreams to you too" was not just clever repartee, it was also my prayer: *God, move in Rose's life.*

Spiritual conversations are like that: they don't just have *utility* (see Paul's logic in Romans 10; if you don't talk about Jesus how are people supposed to call on his name?), they have an *aesthetic* (see Paul's concluding statement: how beautiful are the feet).

Thinking back over your life, what's the most pleasant, interesting, or delightful spiritual conversation you've ever had? Where were you? How did the conversation start?

> How did you feel during the conversation? How did you feel afterward?
> How does it feel to remember, right now, that conversation?

That's what I tasted in the parking lot and in many other conversations. As fearful as I was about spiritual conversations, the reality is they are much more beautiful than I ever guessed. Not only is this the chorus of Scripture, but our new research confirms this reality: spiritual conversations are not as scary and painful and terrible as we've been afraid (see fig. 3.1). Not at all. Let's consider five common myths about spiritual conversations the latest research calls into question.

Five Common Myths About Spiritual Conversations

Myth 1. Spiritual conversations take place in special places, during special moments, by special people. For a variety of reasons, it is fairly common for Christians to assume spiritual conversations are special. They are unlike everyday conversations in many ways, we think. So, they must take place, we figure, in special places (a church, a remote retreat center, someplace where sunbeams are reaching down from heaven), during special moments (a life crisis, an epiphany, when life is at its darkest), and by special people (a pastor, a priest, some Christian who is especially gifted and trained for such conversations).

It turns out we've been figuring this wrong. Not only is Scripture clear that being a witness is something for every Christian but the research reveals spiritual conversations can take place in rather mundane, everyday circumstances. And more often than not, spiritual conversations happen with the regular people who are in your life. In fact, nine out of ten folks who've had a life-changing spiritual conversation say they had it with someone they knew well (31%) or very well (57%). In other words, life change happens because of spiritual conversations with everyday folks.

Interestingly, when asked who they prefer to have spiritual conversations with, Christians *and* non-Christians alike indicated strongly that friends are at the top of the list (see fig. 3.2). Below that was one's spouse, and below that was children. In other words: people want to have spiritual conversations with the everyday folks who are in their everyday life.

I used to labor under the assumption that the pastors of the world were the ones equipped and sent to have spiritual conversations with non-Christians, but I now realize it is everyday folks in everyday settings who are best positioned to have these essential conversations about spiritual matters.

One implication of this research is the importance of Christians being friends with non-Christians. Not only are Christians called to "love our neighbors," but developing trusting friendships with our neighbors is an important precondition for

MY PREFERRED PARTNERS FOR SPIRITUAL CONVERSATIONS

% AMONG U.S. ADULTS; RESPONDENTS COULD CHOOSE UP TO THREE

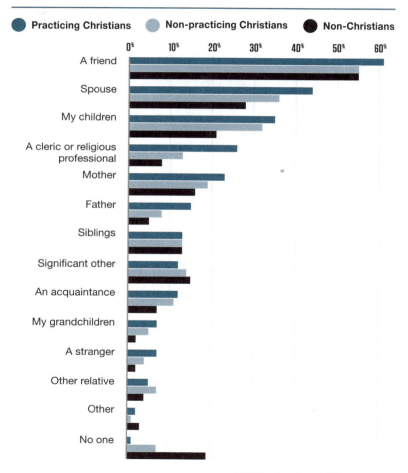

FIGURE 3.2

n=1,070 U.S. adults, June 22–July 13, 2017.

having spiritual conversations. We have to gain a hearing before being able to share our faith.

When I travel and do training with churches and denominations who want to "grow their witness," I always do an exercise early in the training where I ask everyone there to list the two non-Christians in their life that they are closest to. Invariably, there are some present who say they don't know any non-Christians or at least aren't friends with any non-Christians. It turns out this is an important issue. Chatting with Rose was not only a way to bless a somewhat lonely new neighbor, but it also laid the groundwork for possible spiritual conversations.

Developing a friendship with a non-Christian is trickier for some of us than others. The research tells us younger folks on the whole are more likely to have friendships with non-Christians. But regardless of our age, if trust is a prerequisite for spiritual conversations, we all need to consider what we can do to develop more trusting friendships with non-Christians.

> **Who are the two non-Christians you are closest to?**
>
> **How much time in an average week do you spend nurturing a friendship with a non-Christian? How do you feel about that amount?**

Myth 2. Spiritual conversations are serious and sober events. Generally speaking, many of us reluctant conversationalists assume the waters of spiritual conversations are ice-cold—frigid, uncomfortable waters where the conversation tends to be serious and sober. While there are obviously spiritual conversations that get serious (and even sober) at times, it turns out the waters aren't so frigid after all.

In our recent study we pulled back the curtain on these conversations and asked people about a conversation regarding their faith with someone who did not share their faith.

Surprisingly, *laughter* was a common occurrence in these conversations. Not gnashing of teeth, not fisticuffs, but laughter. As you can see in figure 3.3, there is some variation in the occurrence of laughter based on generation, but across the board laughter was a dominant experience.

I remember talking with a new friend who was very cynical about Christians and Christianity. As we got to know each other over lunch one day, he got around to "all the things that annoyed him about Christians."

After mentioning the Crusades and sexual ethics, he got around to his distaste for Christian T-shirts. "Why do you guys always have to wear something about your faith on your shirt? You don't see me putting all my beliefs on my shirt!" What ensued was a hilarious conversation where I told him (as an insider) about all the serious and silly and cheesy Christian T-shirts I had seen over the years. If you've ever considered what atheists might put on their T-shirts to illustrate their

MY MOST RECENT SPIRITUAL CONVERSATION, PART 1

% AMONG U.S. ADULTS WHO HAVE HAD A CONVERSATION ABOUT THEIR FAITH WITH SOMEONE WHO DOES NOT SHARE THEIR FAITH

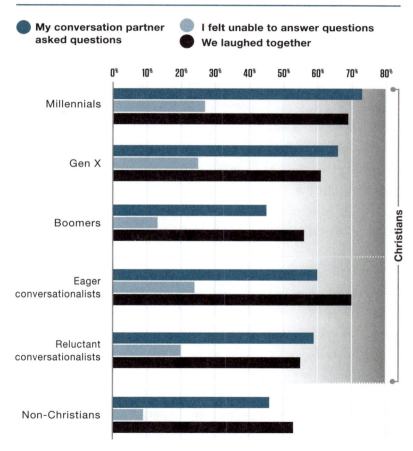

● My conversation partner asked questions
● I felt unable to answer questions
● We laughed together

n= 840 U.S. adults who have had a conversation about their faith, June 22 – July 13, 2017.

FIGURE 3.3

beliefs (or lack thereof), you have a sense of how fun our conversation got that day.

If laughter is a common occurrence in spiritual conversations, maybe these waters aren't so terrible after all. Consider the fact that many Christians who have dived into the waters of spiritual conversation report positive feelings, including peace (71%), joy (55%), and even exhilaration (19%). There are times when negative emotions are experienced, but as you can see in figure 3.4, these are far less common.

Laughter, peace, joy, exhilaration: not exactly the serious and sober affair we perhaps assume. It turns out what God's Word reveals about the delight of witness is accurate. Engaging in spiritual conversations is not only *right* but *good*. The waters of witness are warm and refreshing and enjoyable, not cold and stressful and uncomfortable as we've feared.

Interestingly, psychologists suggest small talk and shallow conversations lead to less happiness than deep conversations.[1] There is something inherently *human* about connecting with others on a deeper level. And there is something inherently *right* about connecting with others on a deep level and sharing about the good news of God's salvation.

> **What about spiritual conversations makes them seem serious or sober?**

EMOTIONS I EXPERIENCE WHEN I TALK ABOUT FAITH

% AMONG U.S. ADULTS WHO HAVE HAD A CONVERSATION ABOUT THEIR FAITH

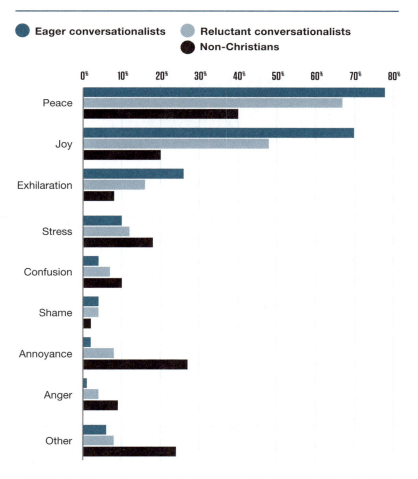

● **Eager conversationalists**　　● **Reluctant conversationalists**
● **Non-Christians**

Peace / Joy / Exhilaration / Stress / Confusion / Shame / Annoyance / Anger / Other

n=840 U.S. adults who have had a conversation about their faith, June 22–July 13, 2017.

FIGURE 3.4

Imagine a conversation between two people of different faiths discussing their faith. What do you imagine that conversation to be like? What emotions do you imagine are present? What's the general tone of the conversation you picture?

List your assumptions about the nature of spiritual conversations, then compare your list with the latest findings.

Myth 3. In a spiritual conversation I need to be able to give the right answers. One fear that keeps many Christians from engaging in more spiritual conversations is the fear of being asked a question about the faith they don't know the answer to. Based on my years of training Christians in having spiritual conversations (and based on my own internal fears), I would say this fear comes partly from our desire to appear knowledgeable (we don't want to be caught with our apologetic pants down, as it were) and partly from our desire to help someone hear the good news (we don't want to get the message wrong).

It is true that questions are a significant part of spiritual conversations. In fact, most Christians (59%) and a plurality of non-Christians (46%; 16% don't know) say their conversation partner asked questions during a spiritual conversation. As you can see in figure 3.3, questions are common in spiritual conversations.

However, all this question asking shouldn't be cause for stress or anxiety. It is actually quite freeing to allow people to ask all their questions without feeling the need to answer each of them crisply and immediately. I once had a new couple come up to me at church with skeptical looks in their eyes. They were new to our church and had heard us announce a new program that was about to start. The program was a practical introduction to Christianity that put an emphasis on providing non-Christians a safe place to ask their questions. This young couple did want to explore the Christian faith, but they weren't so sure about the program. The husband shared their concerns: "You said it's all about asking questions, but we went to a Christian event one time that said it was a place to ask questions, but all they did the whole night was shove answers down our throats. Is this program like that?"

I smiled and pointed to a large display for the program that had a huge question mark on it. "Do you see the display? It doesn't feature an exclamation mark or even a period. It features a question mark. That's what this program is all about. This is a space to wrestle with your questions." That satisfied the couple, and they signed up and came to the program. They had a great time asking all sorts of questions and chewing on those questions and potential answers with the rest of the folks at their table.

Asking lots of questions is a natural part of someone seeking out more about the faith. Often, rather than getting a crisp, memorized answer, non-Christians are more interested in Christians being willing to give them space to ask their questions and being willing to honestly and humbly journey with them toward answers.

In fact, the research indicates it is the process, over time, that leads to people having fruitful spiritual conversations. Seven out of ten people who experienced life change because of a spiritual conversation say the result was actually a result of *multiple* conversations, either with just one person (42%) or with more than one person (27%). The stress we feel to provide the exquisite, exactly on-point answer to a non-Christian's question is of our own creation. Honest and humble journeying with friends in seeking out answers is actually more helpful (and much less stressful).

How much do you feel the pressure to have a ready (and convincing) answer to every question non-Christians have?

What are the top three questions you are most afraid of being asked? What questions about the Christian faith do you feel least prepared to answer?

How does it feel to read that honestly journeying with a friend is often more important than providing a textbook answer? Consider a couple relationships you have with non-Christians: How does the prospect of "honest and humble journeying" with them make you feel?

Myth 4. Most spiritual conversations involve conflict, which ruins everything. I don't know if it was coming of age in a season when high-profile "debates" were being held between Christians and non-Christians about the nature of the Bible, the historicity of accounts about Jesus, the plausibility of creationism, and the like, but I had the impression early on in my life that spiritual conversations often were debates. It was creation *versus* evolution, Jesus Christ as Savior *versus* Jesus Christ as myth. And on and on.

Even some of the apologetic works I read early in life (like Josh McDowell's *Evidence That Demands a Verdict*) gave me the sense that spiritual conversations with non-Christians were primarily about prosecuting a case—and winning.

As a fellow who grew up somewhat allergic to conflict, this turned me off even more to the idea of spiritual conversations with non-Christians. I liked people too much to debate them. It felt a bit too combative for my tastes. I assumed most spiritual conversations would involve conflict, and that conflict would ruin the relationship.

It is true there can be conflict in spiritual conversations. As you can see in figure 3.5, both Christians and non-Christians alike confess to having stirred up conflict while talking about their faith with someone who didn't share their faith.[2]

But what I find fascinating is how relatively low these numbers are. Given the topic (discussing our faith with someone who does not share our faith), I would have expected these numbers to be higher. The relatively low numbers tell us conflict can occur in spiritual conversations, but the vast majority of spiritual conversations are not filled with conflict.

MY MOST RECENT SPIRITUAL CONVERSATION, PART 2

% AMONG U.S. ADULTS WHO HAVE HAD A CONVERSATION ABOUT THEIR FAITH WITH SOMEONE WHO DOES NOT SHARE THEIR FAITH

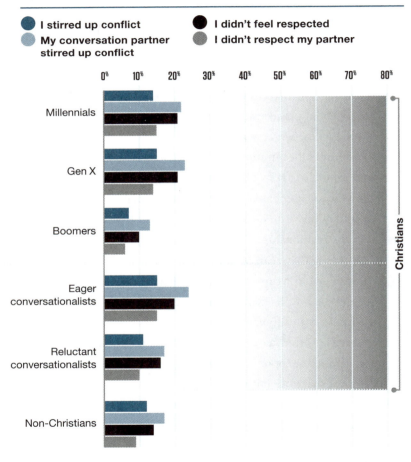

● I stirred up conflict
● My conversation partner stirred up conflict
● I didn't feel respected
● I didn't respect my partner

FIGURE 3.5

n =840 U.S. adults who have had a conversation about their faith, June 22–July 13, 2017.

And where conflict does come up, our in-depth study of "eager conversationalists" (as we'll see in chap. 5) reveals that conflict is not the end of the world. In fact, when analyzing what makes a person glad about having had a spiritual conversation—accounting for conflict, respect, laughing together, how well they knew their conversation partner, when they felt unable to answer questions, and so on—researchers found conflict does not play a significant role in how people feel after the conversation. Conflict, when it does occur, does not in fact ruin everything.

Consider a conflict you experienced while talking about faith. What caused the conflict?

How did you feel during the conflict? How did you feel afterward?

How does it feel, right now, to recall that conflict?

Myth 5. Spiritual conversations are burdensome duties that are, in the end, painful and regrettable. All told, the various assumptions we can at times carry with us about spiritual conversations (they are reserved for special times, places, and people; they are serious and sober; they put us on the spot to provide the right answers; they involve conflict, which ruins everything) can give us a quite skeptical view of spiritual conversations. Many of us wind up viewing spiritual conversations as a necessary duty that proves painful and regrettable.

With that kind of perception, no wonder so many of us remain reluctant conversationalists all through our lives. If we are standing on the dock and the waters of witness look cold and shark-infested—why would we ever willingly dive in?

But what if we have been wrong? What if the waters of witness are warmer and more refreshing and more delightful than we've thought? What if spiritual conversations are actually everyday things? What if they involve plenty of laughter and peace and joy? What if honest journeying rather than exact answers are valued? What if conflict is rarer than we thought and less ruinous than we supposed? What if spiritual conversations aren't so terrible after all?

Spiritual conversations, it turns out, are actually fruitful things. About one-third of all adults in America claim they have personally made a "big change" in their life because of a conversation about faith—a full 35 percent.

And, as far as the most fruitful life change someone could ever experience, many Christians (38%) report that a non-Christian believed in Jesus as their Savior because of a spiritual conversation, as figure 3.6 shows.

It turns out spiritual conversations are as important as they are enjoyable. And they aren't nearly as bad as we have assumed. Perhaps this is why we Christians are so glad once we've jumped into the water.

SOMEONE BELIEVED IN JESUS AS SAVIOR AFTER I TALKED WITH THEM ABOUT MY FAITH

% AMONG SELF-IDENTIFIED CHRISTIANS

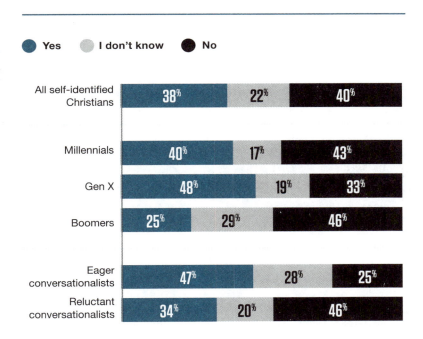

Yes   I don't know   No

	Yes	I don't know	No
All self-identified Christians	38%	22%	40%
Millennials	40%	17%	43%
Gen X	48%	19%	33%
Boomers	25%	29%	46%
Eager conversationalists	47%	28%	25%
Reluctant conversationalists	34%	20%	46%

n=796 U.S. self-identified Christians, June 22–July 13, 2017.

FIGURE 3.6

In fact, a wide majority of Americans, as you can see in figure 3.7, are *glad* about their most recent spiritual conversation with someone who does not share their faith. Among Christians, it's an overwhelming majority (77% among Christians versus 55% of non-Christians).

Rather than regretting their most recent conversation, they are glad. Add in those who *might be* glad, and you can see how wrong we have been about spiritual conversations. The water is much nicer than we had assumed.

> Think of the last spiritual conversation you had with a non-Christian. Are you glad about that conversation? If so, why?
>
> If not, what do you think could have changed the trajectory of that conversation to make it more enjoyable?

Delightful Conversations

The prospect of having a spiritual conversation with a non-Christian is not as scary as we reluctant conversationalists have been assuming. This is what I found out, almost by accident, with my dear friend Rose.

I'll be honest, when Rose first let loose on Christians (as she was setting me and my recycling habits straight), my instinct was to pull back into my shell and fly undercover: *There's no reason for her to know I am a Christian, is there?* Because of all

I AM GLAD ABOUT MY LATEST SPIRITUAL CONVERSATION

% AMONG U.S. ADULTS WHO HAVE HAD A CONVERSATION ABOUT THEIR FAITH WITH SOMEONE WHO DOES NOT SHARE THEIR FAITH

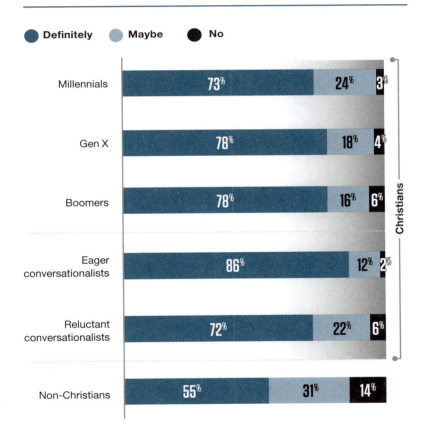

- ● **Definitely** ● **Maybe** ● **No**

Millennials: 73% · 24% · 3%
Gen X: 78% · 18% · 4%
Boomers: 78% · 16% · 6%
Eager conversationalists: 86% · 12% · 2%
Reluctant conversationalists: 72% · 22% · 6%

Christians

Non-Christians: 55% · 31% · 14%

n= 840 U.S. adults who have had a conversation about their faith, June 22–July 13, 2017.

FIGURE 3.7

these assumptions about spiritual conversations I carried around with me, I did *not* want to get into a spiritual conversation with Rose. Her sharp wit alone was reason for me to avoid bringing up my faith.

But over time we became friends. And in the warm light of friendship, it is so plain and natural for the deeper side of life to start to come out. There was a day, for example, when Rose shared about her experience of undergoing hypnosis and how she recovered memories from a previous life, thus seemingly confirming her beliefs in reincarnation. And there was the day when I shared with Rose how God had answered my prayers to deal with my anger and venom toward someone in my life, thus seemingly confirming that God really can heal us. This was simply us as friends getting to know each other. Enjoyable spiritual conversations.

At times we did debate. A few times there was conflict. But mostly we were friends talking about what is most real to us. And the result was peaceful and joyful and funny and, at times, electric—as I experienced while standing out in the snow between our two condos. My eyes were open to God "baring his holy arm," as Isaiah put it, being present and active in our midst. There aren't just two people involved when a Christian has a spiritual conversation—God himself is present.

Looking back, I realize just how important these various conversations were. Some conversations built trust, others deepened our understanding of and empathy with each other. Some conversations involved me sharing about Jesus at work in my life, others involved Rose asking questions about my Christian faith. But regardless of the type of conversation, there was a single thread running through all of them: I was sharing good news. I was, as Isaiah put it, publishing peace, bringing good news of happiness. I was publishing salvation. And you know what? It wasn't nearly as scary as this reluctant conversationalist might have guessed.

This is something eager conversationalists probably already know. You see, the research has revealed a group of Christians who regularly engage in spiritual conversations. These are the Christians who read Isaiah and Paul and have decided to jump right into the waters of spiritual conversations. But what exactly makes these eager conversationalists tick? And what can we reluctant folks learn from them?

WHAT MAKES FOR AN EAGER CONVERSATIONALIST?

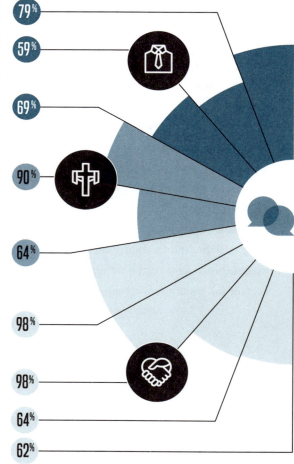

Believe they have a personal responsibility to share their faith with non-believers — **79%**

Have personally experienced a big change in their life due to a conversation about faith — **59%**

Believe God needs Christians to be consistently involved in evangelism in order to convert non-Christians — **69%**

Believe everyone needs their sins forgiven, and forgiveness of sins is only through Jesus' death and resurrection — **90%**

When you die you will go to heaven because you have confessed your sins and have accepted Jesus Christ as your Savior — **64%**

Say faith is very important in their life today — **98%**

Have prayed in the past week — **98%**

Have read the Bible in the past week — **64%**

Have attended church in the past week — **62%**

FIGURE 4.1

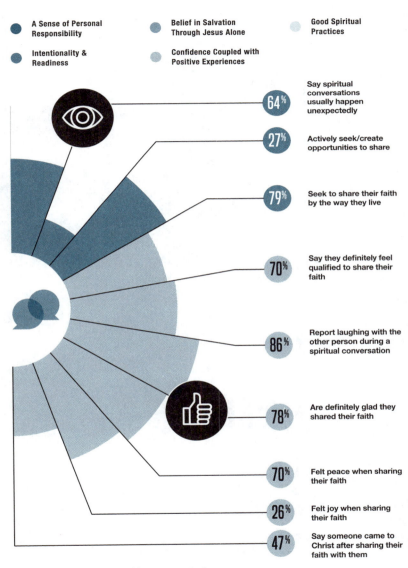

A Sense of Personal Responsibility

Belief in Salvation Through Jesus Alone

Good Spiritual Practices

Intentionality & Readiness

Confidence Coupled with Positive Experiences

64% Say spiritual conversations usually happen unexpectedly

27% Actively seek/create opportunities to share

79% Seek to share their faith by the way they live

70% Say they definitely feel qualified to share their faith

86% Report laughing with the other person during a spiritual conversation

78% Are definitely glad they shared their faith

70% Felt peace when sharing their faith

26% Felt joy when sharing their faith

47% Say someone came to Christ after sharing their faith with them

n=191 U.S. self-identified Christians who qualify as eager conversationalists.

Take up the whole armor of God, that you may be able to withstand in the evil day, and having done all, to stand firm. Stand therefore, having fastened on the belt of truth, and having put on the breastplate of righteousness, and, as shoes for your feet, having put on the readiness given by the gospel of peace. In all circumstances take up the shield of faith, with which you can extinguish all the flaming darts of the evil one; and take the helmet of salvation, and the sword of the Spirit, which is the word of God, praying at all times in the Spirit, with all prayer and supplication.

EPHESIANS 6:13-18

4

Eager Conversationalists

Learning from Those Who Are Still Talking

DOZENS OF EYES ARE STARING UP AT ME where I stand in the front of the church building, sweating. The church building is packed. Many of the children are crammed into the few front pews, the adults fill the rest of the sanctuary. And I, as a college sophomore, am standing in front of all of them, sharing a story of how God has moved in my life.

But that's not why I'm sweating.

This strikes me as interesting in the moment. It's interesting because here I am, a natural-born introvert, talking to a whole room full of people. And the weirdest part is I'm actually enjoying it. I'm sweating simply because it is over one hundred degrees outside and even a little bit hotter inside the cement-block church building here in the jungles of the Yucatan.

We're in Sudzal, a tiny but vibrant Mayan village nestled within the jungles of the Yucatan Peninsula in Mexico. I came here with a team of other college students to partner with the local church of the village in running a summer program for the children of Sudzal. We've been meeting dozens of kids and their parents during the days and sleeping in our hammocks at night. It has been an incredible summer. And I'm amazed at what I am doing and how I feel. I've been talking with people about Jesus. I've been helping lead a summer program, even standing up in a packed church building openly sharing a story about God's work in my life. And it feels different.

It doesn't feel fearful or scary. It isn't uncomfortable or awkward. It feels sort of normal. Exciting, even. Now some of this is surely due to the crosscultural nature of what we're doing. We're living in another country for ten weeks. We're learning a new language and trying new food and getting to know people with completely different backgrounds. As I discovered that first time in the Yucatan—and have experienced again and again ever since—there is something electric about crossing into another culture. It is beautiful and humbling and enlightening and rich.

But that wasn't the only thing going on, and I had a sense of it even as I stood comfortably sharing my story with a room full of people. Of course, giving a presentation is naturally different than being in a one-on-one conversation on a bus. I knew that.

But it wasn't just that the situation I was in felt different. It was that *I* felt different.

I felt comfortable. I felt ready. I felt expectant about what God might do in the situation. I felt keenly aware of my own faults and imperfections and foibles, but equally aware of God's tangible and tender grace for me. I felt compassion for the people around me. And I felt excited to learn from them.

Even as I stood sharing my story, a question began swirling around in my head: *What's happening to me?* I was used to feeling uncomfortable and fearful, withdrawn and quiet. That's who I was. Wasn't it? And yet here I was feeling something different. And something in that moment, and over that whole summer, began slowly but inexorably to disarm a lie that had been secretly living with me most of my life: that I could never be used by God in these ways. That I was always going to be mostly quiet and fearful and awkward.

What's happening to me? Looking back, I realize a couple things were happening that summer. It's clear to me that God was healing me. (And that is always a sublime gift.) It's also clear that my leaders had done a fabulous job of helping outfit me and my teammates for our service that summer.

How did they outfit and prepare us for our service? We had multiple team weekends before ever leaving for the Yucatan. We worked on language skills, did team building, trained for working with children, prayed with each other and for each other, and—this was the part I wasn't expecting—studied Scripture. Our leaders felt studying Scripture together would help prepare us spiritually for what we were going to do in the jungle.

And this spiritual preparation didn't end once we landed in the Yucatan. Our first week in the large capital city of Merida we spent in a simple building complex referred to as the *refugio* (the refuge). We sat around cheap plastic tables studying Peter's first epistle together. We spent time hanging in our hammocks praying and journaling. We also got our *physical* supplies ready for the children. But looking back I realize our leaders knew we not only needed to be fitted out physically for our ministry but also *spiritually*.

And there was something about that spiritual preparation that, combined with God's healing work within me, made it possible for me to stand in front of a packed room and feel expectant rather than fearful.

The Whole Armor of God

This is what Paul was writing about in that famous Ephesians passage in this chapter's epigraph. Paul's injunction to the Christians in Ephesus was to put on the whole armor of God—to be fitted with everything God has for them. The implication is that it is possible to "be strong in the Lord" (a phrase Paul uses just before these verses) if we avail ourselves of everything God has for us. We can be fitted out and prepared for service.

And what has God given us to prepare us for service? According to Paul, truth, righteousness, a gospel of peace, faith, our own salvation, the Holy Spirit, God's Word, prayer. That's the list of armor according to Paul. Looking back at my summer experience in the Yucatan through the lens of Ephesians 6, I realize the answer to that question swirling in the back of my mind: my leaders had helped outfit me spiritually. I felt different because I was "stronger in the Lord."

There was something important about those team meetings prior to leaving for the summer. Something was happening in the *refugio* as we sat around studying the writings of Peter. Something invisible but significant was shifting as we prayed and journaled in our hammocks. We were putting on the armor God had for us. This, in turn, strengthened us. That's a significant part of why I felt different. I was prepared. I was strengthened. I was outfitted— maybe not perfectly and completely but significantly.

And that made me feel different and more ready to be used by God. Using the language of our new research, getting outfitted spiritually was helping me become a more eager conversationalist. My whole life I had been carrying this lie that I wasn't one of those kinds of people: I was introverted, quiet, fearful. But that lie began to be dismantled as I experienced firsthand that being an eager conversationalist wasn't about being a confident extrovert. On the contrary, I was just as introverted as ever. My temperament hadn't changed. Something else had—my spiritual preparedness.

But was this experience unique to me, or is there some real connection between being outfitted as Paul writes about in Ephesians 6 and being an eager conversationalist? This is where our new research becomes so helpful: If it isn't temperament that makes someone an eager conversationalist, what does?

Meet the Eager Conversationalists

As a reminder, the research was focused generally on spiritual conversations with all Americans. But when we isolate all of the self-identified Christians who were surveyed and look at those results, something quite interesting stands out: about three-fourths of all Christians are talking about their faith less than ten times a year, as figure 4.2 illustrates. Remember: that's not talking with a *non-Christian* about faith less than ten times a year but talking with *anyone* about faith (including other Christians) less than ten times a year. These are our reluctant conversationalists.

But the other quarter of all Christians are actually talking about their faith *a lot*. Seventeen percent of them are talking about their faith ten to fifty times a year, and another 10 percent are talking about their faith fifty or more times a year! And here's where the research gets very interesting: if we isolate that 27 percent of

NUMBER OF CONVERSATIONS ABOUT FAITH IN THE PAST YEAR

% AMONG U.S. SELF-IDENTIFIED CHRISTIANS

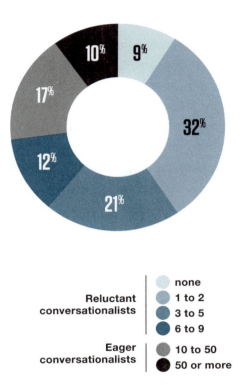

none
1 to 2
3 to 5
6 to 9

Reluctant conversationalists

10 to 50
50 or more

Eager conversationalists

n=796 U.S. self-identified Christians, June 22–July 13, 2017.

FIGURE 4.2

Christians who are still talking about their faith and go back over all the research, carefully examining all their answers to all our questions, we actually find some fascinating similarities.

Generally speaking this 27 percent of us, these eager conversationalists, have a lot in common (see fig. 4.1). But, interestingly, gender, ethnicity, and age aren't among the commonalities.[1] In other words, eager conversationalists come in all types and sizes. This is encouraging. It tells us there is hope for the church. It tells us no group is inherently reluctant—as this introvert learned down in Mexico. It's not age or gender or ethnicity or temperament that shapes how eager someone is to engage in spiritual conversations. It's something else.

What is that something else? What is it that eager conversationalists have in common? It turns out they tend to be spiritually outfitted. This preparedness becomes clear when we look at what they do, what they believe, and how they feel.

What Do Eager Conversationalists Do?

On the whole eager conversationalists are active in their faith. On the surface this tends to make sense: people talk about what is important to them. If our faith is important to us, we will talk about it more. Indeed, eight out of ten eager conversationalists strongly agreed with the phrase "your religious faith is very important in your life today"—82 percent in fact. When reluctant conversationalists were shown the same phrase, only 48 percent of them agreed. In other words, there is a correlation between how important someone's faith is and how likely they are to talk about that faith. Makes sense.

But the difference goes deeper than just feeling our faith is important to us; eager conversationalists are more actively involved in faith practices than reluctant conversationalists.

As you can see in figure 4.3, eager conversationalists pray more, read the Bible more, and attend church services more than reluctant conversationalists. The differences here are statistically significant. They show a correlation between someone's spiritual practices and their willingness to talk about their faith. In one sense this shouldn't surprise us: the more *everyday* someone's faith is, the more they will tend to talk about it in *everyday* situations. Not too surprising.

Paul would undoubtedly not be surprised by this either. Paul saw these activities (praying and studying the Word of God) as armor. These spiritual practices are part of how we are outfitted for the labors God has for us, including being a witness. This is, in a sense, exactly what I experienced in the Yucatan. I didn't have the language to describe what was happening at the time, but I intuitively felt the difference. All that time spent praying, worshiping, and studying God's Word had outfitted me for service. I became "stronger in the Lord."

EAGER VS. RELUCTANT: ENGAGEMENT IN SPIRITUAL PRACTICES DURING THE PAST WEEK

% AMONG U.S. SELF-IDENTIFIED CHRISTIANS

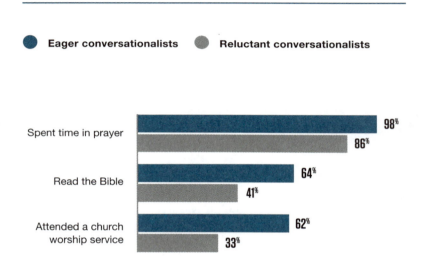

● Eager conversationalists ● Reluctant conversationalists

Spent time in prayer
98%
86%

Read the Bible
64%
41%

Attended a church worship service
62%
33%

n=796 U.S. self-identified Christians, June 22–July 13, 2017.

FIGURE 4.3

It is not surprising then that those who are more active in the mission of sharing the good news of Jesus with the people around them are folks who are more active in activities that spiritually fit them for the battle God has before them. In the same way that a healthy diet makes us feel healthier physically and more ready to face our day, so too a healthy spiritual diet makes us feel healthier spiritually and more ready to face our mission.

How strongly do you agree with the statement "your religious faith is very important in your life today"?

How often do you attend worship services during an average month?

How often do you read the Bible in an average week?

How often do you pray during an average day?

How does trying to quantify your spiritual practices make you feel?

What Do Eager Conversationalists Believe?

An integral part of our armor that Paul talks about is the truth that God has given us. Paul encourages the believers in Ephesus to "fasten on the belt of truth" and reminds them that the sword they have been given is the Word of God. There is something about God's revealed truth that not only *protects us* (the belt held the whole outfit of armor together in the ancient world) but also *equips us* to engage in the battles God has for us (the sword is the only weapon in Paul's description).

It is not too surprising that eager conversationalists are on the whole more tightly holding to God's Word than their reluctant counterparts. In chapter two we considered the sobering research that seems to indicate reluctant conversationalists' beliefs tend to look more like the world's and less like what is taught in the Bible. Here we consider the other side of that coin: eager conversationalists tend to have biblical beliefs—their belt of truth is buckled.

As you can see in figure 4.4, eager conversationalists are nearly twice as likely as reluctant conversationalists to believe that "the Bible is totally accurate in all the principles it teaches," and this high view of the Bible bears itself out in specific doctrines.

For example, eager conversationalists are more likely than reluctant conversationalists to believe "everyone needs to have their sins forgiven" (68% versus 41%). And we find similar differences when we drill into specific beliefs about life after death.

Barna asks questions to determine whether someone holds an orthodox, moralist, or universalist view of the afterlife. An *orthodox* view of the afterlife is the traditional biblical teaching that when a person dies they go to heaven because they've confessed their sins and have faith in Jesus as their Savior. A *moralist* view of the afterlife is that heaven is something a person earns through human effort. A *universalist* view of the afterlife is that everyone will go to heaven because God won't let anyone perish. Eager conversationalists? They are much more likely to

EAGER VS. RELUCTANT: BELIEFS

% STRONGLY AGREE AMONG U.S.
SELF-IDENTIFIED CHRISTIANS

 **Eager conversationalists**   **Reluctant conversationalists**

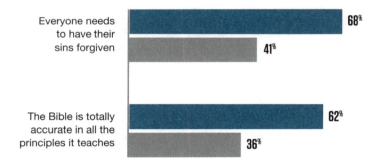

Everyone needs
to have their
sins forgiven — 68%, 41%

The Bible is totally
accurate in all the
principles it teaches — 62%, 36%

n=796 U.S. self-identified Christians, June 22–July 13, 2017.

FIGURE 4.4

hold the biblical, orthodox view of the afterlife than reluctant conversationalists—64 percent to 49 percent (see fig. 4.5).

On one level this makes practical sense: if we believe faith in Jesus matters eternally, we have more internal motivation to share about Jesus with others. But the eager conversationalists' habit of regular Bible reading, combined with the specific beliefs they derive from the Bible (about the Bible, sin, eternal life) point to a broader reality: their truth belt tends to be more securely buckled.

I'm not sure I could have pointed to specific doctrines I garnered from Peter's first epistle while sitting around those cheap plastic tables in the *refugio* that made me feel readier to stand up and share with others about my own faith that summer in the Yucatan. But I am convinced there was a relationship between how much time I spent in God's Word and how I felt that summer. Being in God's Word—with our spiritual belt buckled—helps us stand taller, more sure, healthier.

> What do you believe about heaven? About who gets into heaven? About how people get into heaven?
>
> Describe how "buckled" your "belt of truth" is (not at all, loosely, tightly).

How Do Eager Conversationalists Feel?

In a few places the research probed into the area of feelings. One area of feelings we already considered in chapter three was what

EAGER VS. RELUCTANT:
LIFE AFTER DEATH

% AMONG U.S. SELF-IDENTIFIED CHRISTIANS

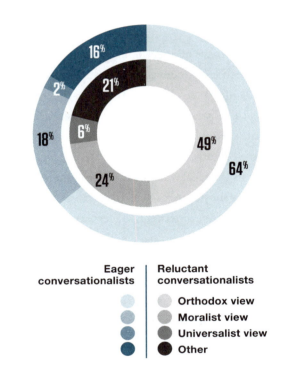

16%
2%
21%
18%
6%
49%
64%
24%

Eager conversationalists

Reluctant conversationalists

- Orthodox view
- Moralist view
- Universalist view
- Other

n = 796 U.S. self-identified Christians, June 22–July 13, 2017.

FIGURE 4.5

emotions people experience when they talk about their faith. There we noted the three most dominant emotions experienced by Christians when they talk about their faith are peace, joy, and exhilaration.

But as we revisit those findings, notice in figure 4.6 the marked difference between eager conversationalists and reluctant conversationalists. Our eager conversationalists are more likely to experience peace, joy, and exhilaration, and they are less likely to experience stress, confusion, annoyance, and anger. There is a correlation between how often someone talks about their faith and the emotions they feel when talking about their faith.

What exactly is the nature of that correlation? It could simply be that the more we do something, the less stressful it becomes. Or it could be that folks who have a negative experience in a spiritual conversation just decide to not enter into as many spiritual conversations.

In considering how the causality works here, it is interesting to note that eager conversationalists are more prepared for spiritual conversations. Or at least they *feel* prepared. A full 65 percent of eager conversationalists said they "definitely" feel qualified to share their faith (see fig. 4.7). By contrast, only 40 percent of reluctant conversationalists definitely feel qualified. As you can see, only 4 percent of eager conversationalists explicitly don't feel qualified. This is significant.

EMOTIONS I EXPERIENCE WHEN I TALK ABOUT FAITH

% AMONG U.S. ADULTS WHO HAVE HAD A CONVERSATION ABOUT THEIR FAITH

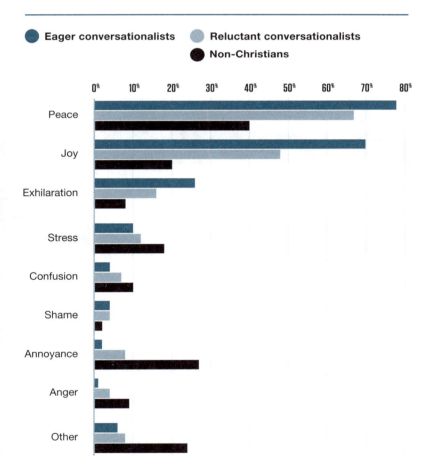

● Eager conversationalists　● Reluctant conversationalists
● Non-Christians

n=840 U.S. adults who have had a conversation about their faith, June 22–July 13, 2017.

FIGURE 4.6

EAGER VS. RELUCTANT:
I FEEL QUALIFIED TO SHARE MY FAITH

% AMONG U.S. SELF-IDENTIFIED CHRISTIANS

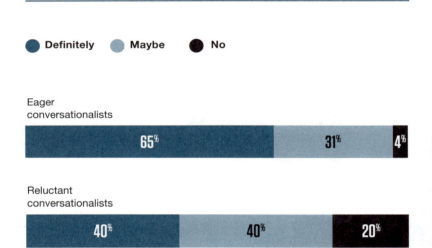

● Definitely   ● Maybe   ● No

Eager
conversationalists

65%   31%   4%

Reluctant
conversationalists

40%   40%   20%

n = 796 U.S. self-identified Christians. June 22–July 13, 2017.

FIGURE 4.7

Twenty-five years ago, 77 percent of all Christians felt their own church did a good job of training people to share their faith. Today, that number has dropped to 57 percent. Christians in general feel their churches are not equipping them to talk about their faith in Jesus. In general, feeling ill-equipped for a task may make us reluctant to attempt that task. So, it stands to reason then that the more equipped and prepared we feel, the more positive our experience will be, all things being equal.

This is what I felt in Mexico: my leaders prepared us for what we were going to do. In fact, they led me through an exercise of reflecting on a personal faith story and translating the trickier words into Spanish *before we ever got to Mexico*. So, when I was asked, spur of the moment, to stand up in that packed, hot church building and share a story about God's work in my life, I was prepared. I *felt* prepared. And so, it didn't feel as scary or stressful or awkward.

I've taken many college students down to Mexico since that first summer, and every time I make sure they prepare to share a faith story of their own—just in case they are asked. I have experienced firsthand how being prepared changes the game. This is especially true, I have seen, when it comes to feeling prepared to share our own faith.

I'll never forget sharing a simple diagram—a four-circle diagram that illustrates the Christian story (see fig. 4.8)—with my friend Michelle, a shy, diminutive college student who had spent the first semester of her freshman year avoiding the other people on her college campus.[2] Michelle avoided others in her dorm, in class, and even in the cafeteria kitchen at her work-study job. She was just so shy and out of her element on the large campus.

Then one day I happened to share this simple four-circle diagram with Michelle—not to equip her in how to talk about her faith but simply because I thought it was cool. A week later we were meeting again, and Michelle mentioned she had been thinking about that diagram and had found it helpful. In fact, she told me, three people in the kitchen at her work-study job had found it interesting too.

I was shocked. *Shy Michelle had shared the faith with three people?* Eyes wide, I asked Michelle, "Have you ever shared the gospel with someone before?" She looked confused. She had never shared the gospel with anyone, she assured me. She was too scared to do that. When I explained that by walking her friends through the diagram, she had, indeed, shared the gospel with them, Michelle was thrilled.

Fascinated, I asked, "Michelle, why didn't you think talking your friends through the diagram was sharing the gospel?" Her answer has stuck with me ever since: "Because it felt so natural. I assumed it wasn't sharing the gospel unless it felt awkward and hard."

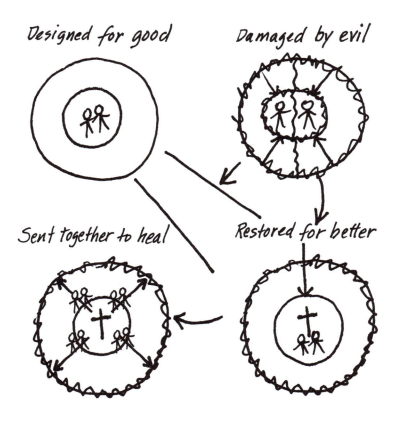

Designed for good

Damaged by evil

Sent together to heal

Restored for better

FIGURE 4.8

Michelle was equipped with a simple tool. And being equipped, feeling prepared in that way, made her experience of the conversations more enjoyable and natural. So enjoyable that she assumed it must not be evangelism! This is exactly what I felt in the Yucatan. I was prepared and so I felt different. And this is the experience of many eager conversationalists: they feel prepared to talk about their faith, and they have more enjoyable conversations.

So, how do we best get equipped for spiritual conversations? I have personal experience with a few resources that help people be better equipped to talk about their faith—like James Choung's *True Story*, my and Doug Schaupp's *I Once Was Lost*, Rick Mattson's *Faith Is Like Skydiving*, and many, many others. Lutheran Hour Ministries' research with Barna has led LHM to develop three online courses based on the research to help us all better prepare for spiritual conversations. These courses are interactive, available online, and absolutely free. One of these courses, "Prepared to Respond: The Spiritual Conversation Curve," is specifically designed to equip people to talk about their faith.[3]

There are many such resources out there. The point here is what it feels like to be prepared and how that preparation corresponds to an increase in spiritual conversations. I think, for example, of the great fruit I have seen within many Christian communities that take seriously the "five thresholds" tool.[4] Doug Schaupp, who led the team that first developed this equipping tool, has described how InterVarsity Christian Fellowship has seen a drastic increase in spiritual conversations due in part to a simple commitment to equip students to talk about their faith, primarily by coaching them in the "five thresholds." Being equipped makes a difference.

> **Describe how qualified you feel to share about your faith (definitely, maybe, not at all).**
>
> **What training have you received about how to talk about your faith (reading a book, taking a class, being mentored)?**
>
> **What equipping does your Christian community offer in this area?**

Getting to Know the Eager Conversationalists

The research gives us a great overview of the average eager conversationalist: they actively practice spiritual disciplines (like praying, reading the Bible, and going to church); they believe what the Bible teaches about witness and salvation and the afterlife; and they feel prepared to talk about their faith. The net result is they have a more enjoyable and more natural experience in spiritual conversations.

In the Yucatan I got a taste of this experience: my leaders had me engaging in more spiritual disciplines than I was used to, I was spending lots of time in prayer, and I had been decently prepared for what I was being asked to do.

And, as I realized halfway through sharing about God's work in my life with a room full of people, I felt different. When I returned to the United States and to my college campus at the end of the summer, that feeling didn't go away. Of course, it felt different being back in my own country, on my familiar turf. That electric surge that came from living crossculturally and learning from people who were different from me was no longer there. But I still felt different.

I was asked to lead a Bible study in the dorms on my campus that fall, and I *wanted* to. I felt ready to. I found myself going door to door to meet people on campus, initiating with new people, having lots of conversations (even some spiritual conversations) with the people I met. And it simply wasn't as awkward as it once might have been for me. In fact, things felt surprisingly easier than the summer experience because we all spoke the same language!

I was outfitted in Mexico—putting on more of the armor of God than I had ever done before. And that, as Paul knew, makes a difference in helping us to be "stronger in the Lord."

This is the experience of eager conversationalists too, as revealed in the research findings. What we learned about them tells us quite a bit about why they are having more spiritual conversations and why they are able to enjoy the ones they have.

But how exactly do eager conversationalists engage in those conversations? And is there anything we can learn from the conversational habits of eager conversationalists? That's what we turn our attention to next.

WHY DON'T YOU HAVE SPIRITUAL CONVERSATIONS MORE OFTEN?

Religious conversations always seem to create tension or arguments — **28%**

I'm not religious and don't care about these kinds of topics — **23%**

Cannot recall / not sure — **21%**

I'm put off by how religion has been politicized — **17%**

I don't feel like I know enough to talk about religious or spiritual topics — **17%**

I don't want to be known as a religious person — **7%**

FIGURE 5.1

I don't know how to talk about religious or spiritual topics without sounding weird **6%**

I'm afraid people will see me as a fanatic or extremist **5%**

I'm embarrassed by the way religious language has been used in popular culture **5%**

I've been hurt by religious conversations in the past **4%**

Religious language and jargon feels cheesy or outdated **4%**

n=522 | May 15-19, 2017 | from a Barna study conducted for the book *Learning to Speak God from Scratch* by Jonathan Merritt.

FIGURE 5.2

Now who is there to harm you if you are zealous for what is good? But even if you should suffer for righteousness' sake, you will be blessed. Have no fear of them, nor be troubled, but in your hearts honor Christ the Lord as holy, always being prepared to make a defense to anyone who asks you for a reason for the hope that is in you; yet do it with gentleness and respect, having a good conscience, so that, when you are slandered, those who revile your good behavior in Christ may be put to shame. For it is better to suffer for doing good, if that should be God's will, than for doing evil.

1 PETER 3:13-17

Everyday Conversations

Exploring Four Simple Conversational Habits

So, it's late spring, just a few weeks left in my junior year of college, and everyone in my religion class is looking at me. It's a small class—fewer than ten students have taken History of Christian Thought II—but that doesn't lessen how awkward it feels to have everyone staring at me. The staring didn't end quickly. As it turned out, everyone stared at me as I faced three separate, significant moments that afternoon.

Three Significant Moments

*Moment 1. **Will I be honest about my faith and its implications?*** I don't even remember how the class got off topic (in a small class with a fair amount of class discussion this was not uncommon), but a few moments earlier the topic had gotten around to the sexual ethics within Christianity, and Professor Steve, a new professor at our school in his early thirties, had asked the class a very personal question: *How many of you believe in waiting to have sex until marriage?* That question created something of a moment for me.

You see I was attending a liberal private university, taking a class in a liberal religion department. It had become apparent over the course of the semester that the young professor teaching us about Christian thought was not a Christian and viewed believing Christians as somewhere between quaint and offensive. Most students in the class followed suit.

So, on this spring day when Professor Steve asked his question, it was less of a conversation starter and more of a cynical hypothetical question. He asked the question with the same tone and inflection you would ask, "I mean, how many of you have two heads?" He was not expecting an answer.

And that created a moment for me. I'm no lover of conflict. I don't overly enjoy being embarrassed. All I had to do was hold my breath for a few beats and the hypothetical question would pass and Professor Steve would move on. This was the first moment I faced that afternoon: Will I be honest about my faith and its implications? *How many of you believe in waiting to have sex until marriage?* I did. And so I raised my hand.

This wasn't a brave, fight-against-the-system hand raised high with pride. My elbow still on the desk, I tentatively lifted my hand ten inches or so. Professor Steve's eyes got wide. He smiled. I could imagine the thought bubble above his head: *Oh goodie, another naive Christian youth to disabuse of the vestiges of their childhood religion.* And just like that he launched into a heady discourse about process theology and how the Bible was really intended to be read and what God is really all about and how static conceptions of morality or sexual ethics are really a misreading of God and the Bible.

He was serious and capable and eloquent and quoting (from memory) lots of learned scholars. He was passionate. And all my classmates were nodding and smiling. Eventually, he brought his mini-lecture to a close, and that's when all heads swiveled back to me. All eyes on me. Fewer than ten students, but still. An awkward moment.

Moment 2. Will I relent and admit I have been mistaken? In the wake of my professor's mini-lecture, I'm not sure how to respond. Should I stick to my guns? Debate the professor? Storm out of the room? Or is God doing something else here? Is this an awkward moment to be escaped or a God moment to be entered into? Is this an academic conversation alone or had we meandered closer to a spiritual conversation? I had a sense in the moment, a light nudge from the Spirit, that I should lean into the moment. So, I did.

The class and professor were waiting for me to repent of my naive moral views and evolve with them into the rarified air of process theology. Or perhaps they were waiting for me to punch back with some embarrassing apologetic for old-fashioned ethics. Instead, I leaned into the moment by being honest. And vulnerable.

"If you want to understand what I believe, you'd have to know what I experienced in high school." And just like that I launched into a transparent telling of my own story: how I had ignored God's clear guidance on sexual practice in high school and the fallout that occurred because of that. I shared the deep, personal reflection I had done after that fiasco, comparing the realities of life to the wisdom in God's Word. I shared how this revealed for me the kindness of God giving his people a "blessed no" when it came to sexual expression outside of the marriage bed. I shared how God's clear words were guiding me and my current girlfriend and how much more sane things were now than what I had experienced in high school. I even got a little honest about my own temptations and how they made me glad for God's "blessed no."

I wasn't trying to be persuasive or argumentative. Just talking about my own life with God. This was becoming a natural enough thing for me. What was new was the location: talking about my own life with God *in class*. I was getting used to having spiritual conversations in Bible study or in church or with a few friends who shared my faith. This was different: having a spiritual conversation in an everyday context. And what happened next has remained with me as a reminder that when God nudges me to lean into a moment, I should.

Professor Steve didn't respond for a few beats. All the eyes were now back on him. And when he finally spoke, the professorial tone was gone from his voice. He didn't quote any erudite scholars. He talked about his own life. "Well, that sounds great. But what do you do if you are in your early thirties and there's no prospect in sight, and you are years from being married?" His tone was humble, introspective, maybe a little sad or angry. No more lofty theories to hide behind. No more debate. This was him. And me. And my third moment.

Moment 3. Will I lean into this honest spiritual conversation to take it further? I could ask him more questions about his story: Have there been prospects in the past? Is there some sadness or anger about the lack of a woman in his life? How is it working out engaging in sexual expressions outside the context of marriage? And so on.

I could empathize with him: Exploring similarities in our stories. Sharing more about my own seasons without a prospect and how the "blessed no" felt in that context. Exploring the context and nature of the texts in the Bible that express the "blessed no" and the rationale given in those texts.

I could tentatively suggest ways that God could be involved in his own story: Walking by his side in the midst of waiting and struggling. Having him handle God's Word as part of his profession. Offering him understanding and kindness in the midst of the heavy load he is carrying and struggling with.

I could reschedule, offering to talk after class or during office hours since it can be hard to talk about personal things in a professional setting.

How did I respond to moment 3? I wish I could say I responded wisely and bravely, that our spiritual conversation continued and more people in the class started to get honest about their own stories, that I had a chance to see God move in powerful ways right there in the classroom. The reality is less glorious than that. At least less explicitly so. I said, simply, "That sounds hard."

And the moment passed. And Steve got professorial again. And that's it. At least that's all that I got to see.

Responding with Gentleness and Respect

Looking back, I'm unsure of what exactly to make of this in-class conversation. Part of me feels I did well in the first two moments God gave me but bailed out of the third moment. So, some regret. There's part of me that wonders what God eventually did with the few seeds I cast that day. How did God use those simple words and the heralding of God's Word in the life of that young professor? So, some hope. And finally, there's part of me that is upset that I was put in such an awkward, unfair situation as a Christian in a class setting. So, some frustration too.

As we discussed earlier, the reality is we are living in an age when the gospel is "out of season," so such potentially awkward, potentially beautiful moments are not uncommon. In fact, Peter's brazen and sturdy words from his first letter that we have as this chapter's epigraph do a decent job of preparing us for moments exactly like this.

Peter is writing from Rome and sending this letter to Christians who've been dispersed into five areas of Asia Minor. These Christians are clearly living through a season when the gospel was "out of season." In fact, from Peter's letter it becomes clear these Christians are being treated poorly because of their faith. It is unclear whether they are facing *physical* persecution, but clearly they are facing verbal abuse and some manner of discrimination because of their faith in Jesus.

In a sense my awkward moment shouldn't have surprised me or caught me off-balance. I was studying in a secular university in a secular religion department during the beginnings of our current postmodern, post-Christian season in American life. Should I have been surprised that my own beliefs, my own lifestyle, would be seen as out of sync?

Rather than be afraid or troubled or surprised, Peter encourages these Asia Minor Christians to be prepared. Not with angry, clever debate moves, but with a gentle, respectful defense for the hope they have within them. There are really two aspects to being prepared, according to Peter. The first relates to content: "Always [be] prepared to make a defense to anyone who asks you for a reason for the hope that is in you" (1 Peter 3:15).

Peter wants these Christians to be prepared with an answer, a defense for the work God is doing in their lives. They have hope that comes from their life in Jesus. Peter wants them to have ready words for the people around them who question their beliefs and lifestyle. It is important to be prepared with content. Before that spring day in class, I had talked with other Christian friends about my own story with sexuality and how God had been at work in me in that area of life. It turns out those spiritual conversations with other Christians helped prepare me for answering the questions and perplexed looks of my class-mates on that day. Interestingly, a few of the reasons people don't have more spiritual conversations these days have to do with content, as you can see in figures 5.1 and 5.2.

But Peter is clear we need to be prepared with more than mere content to explain ourselves. We need to also be prepared with, well, a loving posture. After Peter encourages these be-lievers to be zealous for what is good, to be righteous (do the right thing), and to be prepared with an explanation for their life in Jesus, he then encourages them to do this with the right posture: "Do it with gentleness and respect, having a good conscience, so that, when you are slandered, those who revile your good behavior in Christ may be put to shame. For it is better to suffer for doing good, if that should be God's will, than for doing evil" (1 Peter 3:15-17).

Even when persecuted, we are to be gentle. Even when being maligned, we are to be respectful. Even if we are unfairly singled out, we are to behave in such a way that we have a good conscience at the end of the day.

It is quite possible I fumbled my third moment that spring day in college—not quite prepared enough to take a tender spiritual conversation further. But looking back I am glad God had prepared me to respond to the awkward feeling-a-little-bit-persecuted moment rather than fearfully avoid it. And I am glad he had prepared me to respond with gentleness and respect rather than debate and anger. Note in figures 5.1 and 5.2 that most of the reasons people don't have more spiritual conversations relate to posture rather than content.

This is something of what Peter wanted the Christians living in Asia Minor to get and is something the research suggests eager conversationalists have gotten as well. Consider a few of the conversational habits eager conversationalists have. These habits illustrate what it looks like to live into Peter's invitation in our own day and age. These are habits we can all learn from.

Habits to Learn From

Habit 1. Eager conversationalists look for and expect spiritual conversations in everyday life. In chapter three we explored the myth that "spiritual conversations take place in special places, during special moments, by special people." The research actually suggests spiritual conversations usually take place in familiar, everyday settings. Like a bus. Or at work. Or in a classroom. People today want to have spiritual conversations with people they know—not with religious professionals in a religious setting. Spiritual conversations happen in real life.

In chapter four we considered the fact that we see a correlation in eager conversationalists between spiritual practices and willingness to talk about the faith. The more *everyday* someone's faith is, the more they will tend to talk about their faith in *everyday* situations. And this is what eager conversationalists do.

It's also meaningful that eager conversationalists are less likely to view spiritual conversations as something we accidentally fall into. They are more likely to actively seek opportunities to share their faith, as you can see in figure 5.3.

Think of Paul's posture: "At the same time, pray also for us, that God may open to us a door for the word, to declare the mystery of Christ, on account of which I am in prison" (Colossians 4:3). Paul doesn't think he'll just happen upon a chance to share about Jesus—he believes God is active all around him. Paul

OPPORTUNITIES TO SHARE FAITH, BY NUMBER OF CONVERSATIONS

% AMONG SELF-IDENTIFIED CHRISTIANS WHO HAVE HAD A CONVERSATION ABOUT THEIR FAITH

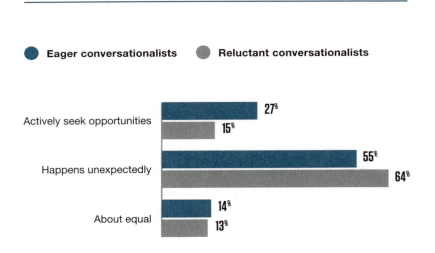

● Eager conversationalists ● Reluctant conversationalists

Actively seek opportunities
27%
15%

Happens unexpectedly
55%
64%

About equal
14%
13%

n= 796 U.S. self-identified Christians, June 22 - July 13, 2017.

FIGURE 5.3

believes God can "open a door" for him to share about Jesus at any moment, so he is praying for and looking for these moments.

In my recent work with Doug Schaupp and Val Gordon, we studied "conversion communities."[1] What's a conversion community? Imagine a church where people are coming to faith on a regular basis, where most months there is someone confessing faith in Jesus. That's a conversion community. Doug, Val, and I set about to locate and study some of these churches and communities to see what they had in common with each other. Among our findings was this: in communities where new people are coming to faith on a regular basis, the Christians there expect "God moments" to happen in everyday life.

A God moment is simply a moment where we see God actively at work in the people around us and sense God is opening a door for us to be a part of his work in their life. It turns out conversion communities are filled with people who expect God to be at work in the world around them, including the non-Christians around them.

In other words, there is something healthy (and even fruitful) about Christians who expect God to break into everyday life and be at work in even the most mundane circumstances. Like on a bus. Or at work. Or in a classroom. This is a habit eager conversationalists have. If you expect God moments, then you are more on the lookout for them, even looking for small hints that

God may be at work: a quick tear, an earnest question, a heartfelt response, a nudge from God to initiate.

We have a sense of this in Peter's encouragement to "always be prepared." You never know when someone may ask about the hope that is in you and God may nudge you to explain that hope, even in somewhat hostile environments. You never know when God may open a door. Eager conversationalists are in the habit of looking for these God moments.

I was sort of blindsided back in that classroom—I wasn't expecting a spiritual conversation to blossom in such soil. I wasn't watching for an open door that afternoon. But I had become a bit more prepared for spiritual conversations over the previous couple years. Preparation that pays off when God opens these doors for us.

> **How expectant are you for open doors to spiritual conversations? Describe a time when you felt subtly nudged by God to lean into a moment or a conversation.**
>
> **How prepared do you feel to talk about your faith and Christian lifestyle?**
>
> **Describe your default posture when you are talking with non-Christians about faith (gentleness and respect, anger and defensiveness, something else entirely).**

Habit 2. Eager conversationalists pursue and initiate spiritual conversations. Not only are eager conversationalists in the habit of expecting and looking for spiritual conversations, they also go a step further and seek to *spark* spiritual conversations. Christians as a whole are less likely than they were twenty-five years ago to believe talking about their faith happens unexpectedly (down from 75% to 61%) and much more likely to believe they should be seeking and creating opportunities to share about their faith (up from 11% to 19%), as you can see in figure 5.4.

This makes sense: as the gospel has become more "out of season," we intuitively sense we need to be proactive in talking about our faith rather than waiting for it to unexpectedly come up in conversation.

It would seem eager conversationalists are even more convinced of this than the average Christian. Whereas 19 percent of all Christians who've talked about their faith with a non-Christian believe they need to seek and create such opportunities, a full 77 percent of eager conversationalists believe they have a personal responsibility to share their faith with nonbelievers. And 68 percent of them believe God needs Christians to be consistently involved in evangelism in order to reach non-Christians.

This willingness to try to spark spiritual conversations from time to time is a conversational habit. It's one thing to expect and be on the lookout for spiritual conversations in everyday life; it's another thing to respond to God's nudging by attempting

THEN & NOW:
OPPORTUNITIES TO SHARE FAITH

% AMONG CHRISTIANS WHO HAVE HAD A CONVERSATION ABOUT THEIR FAITH

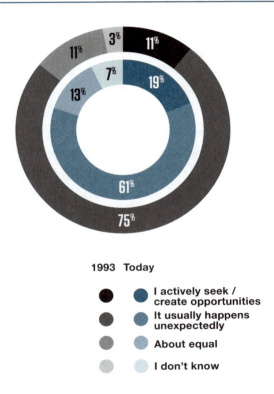

11% 3% 11%
7% 19%
13%
61%
75%

1993 Today

● ● I actively seek / create opportunities

● ● It usually happens unexpectedly

● ● About equal

● ● I don't know

1993: n=446 Christians who have had a conversation about their faith, August 14 - 20, 1993;
Today: n=796 Christians who have had a conversation about their faith, June 22–July 13, 2017.

FIGURE 5.4

to initiate such a conversation. When eager conversationalists sense an open door, they are more likely to walk through it.

This doesn't mean awkwardly inserting Christian non sequiturs into conversations ("Speaking of your new car, if you were hit by a bus tonight, do you know where you would spend eternity?"), as we will see in the next habit. But it does mean tentative, hopeful moments in a conversation that eager conversationalists are willing to explore to see if God might use them to take the conversation deeper ("When you were talking about your weekend, you seemed pretty reflective. Anything big happen for you and your family?").

Back in that classroom, this was the nudge I felt from God to get honest and vulnerable about my own story. That honesty was a way of leaning into the conversation to see if the everyday moment might in actuality also be a God moment. In the end, it was. God used my comments to do something within the heart of my professor—getting beyond his lofty theories to his hurting heart. But if my own vulnerability didn't spark anything, that's okay. In *Breaking the Huddle* we explored different ways active witnesses lean into conversations to see what God might be up to, and we found there is something prayerful and hopeful and tentative about these potential sparks, quite the opposite of something forced and awkward and aggressive.

Christians have been known to initiate such conversations in all sorts of everyday places. As the research indicates, folks have experienced big life change because of spiritual conversations that happened in all sorts of everyday places, including the digital spaces of life (see fig. 5.5).

A significant amount of all adult Americans who've experienced big life change because of a spiritual conversation list digital spaces among the places those conversations took place, including on the phone (39%), via texting or chatting (29%), and even email (24%). It doesn't get much more everyday than that!

The habit of looking to initiate or spark a spiritual conversation translates into many everyday circumstances and environments. Eager conversationalists seem to epitomize this readiness that keeps them on their toes in conversation. Perhaps this is part of what Paul was getting at in Ephesians 6 when he characterized the readiness that comes from the gospel as a pair of shoes for the Christian's feet. Eager conversationalists have these gospel sneakers on—not going through life flat-footed but on the balls of their feet, ready to be used, looking for places to spark a spiritual conversation.

> Think of the last time you tried to spark a spiritual conversation. How did it go? How did it feel?
>
> What do you think is important to keep in mind so that you can spark a spiritual conversation while still being gentle and respectful?

INTERACTIONS THAT LED TO MY BIG LIFE CHANGE

% AMONG U.S. ADULTS WHO EXPERIENCED A BIG CHANGE AFTER A SPIRITUAL CONVERSATION; RESPONDENTS COULD SELECT ALL THAT APPLY

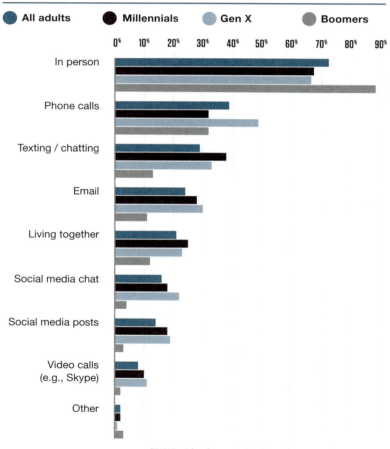

● All adults   ● Millennials   ● Gen X   ● Boomers

In person

Phone calls

Texting / chatting

Email

Living together

Social media chat

Social media posts

Video calls (e.g., Skype)

Other

n=374 U.S. adults who report a big change after a spiritual conversation.
June 22–July 13, 2017.

FIGURE 5.5

Habit 3. Eager conversationalists are open to sharing their faith in a wide variety of ways.

Perhaps many of us have seen someone awkwardly ply the same evangelistic device in a variety of conversations regardless of where the conversation was or where their conversation partners were in their journey ("Speaking of today's traffic, if you were hit by a bus tonight . . ."). There seems to be something a bit ungentle and even disrespectful about such an approach.

The research shows eager conversationalists do not witness a single way, rather they are open to sharing their faith using various approaches. As you can see in figure 5.6, eager conversationalists are more likely than reluctant conversationalists to use a variety of approaches in a spiritual conversation, seeming to indicate adaptability on their part. Likewise, they are more likely to use a wide variety of *mediums* for a spiritual conversation (face-to-face conversation, email, phone call, text, etc.), again seeming to suggest adaptability.

It is meaningful that right after Paul asked the Colossians to pray for "open doors" to share about Jesus, he invited them to be wise and thoughtful about how they themselves walked through those open doors: "Walk in wisdom toward outsiders, making the best use of the time. Let your speech always be gracious, seasoned with salt, so that you may know how you ought to answer each person" (Colossians 4:5-6).

EAGER VS. RELUCTANT: APPROACHES TO FAITH-SHARING

% AMONG U.S. SELF-IDENTIFIED CHRISTIANS, RESPONDENTS COULD SELECT ALL THAT APPLY

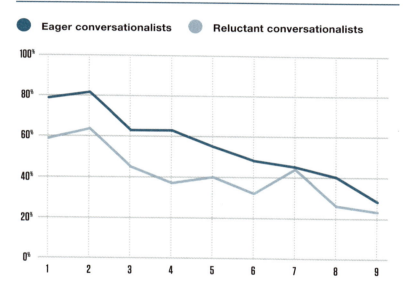

- **Eager conversationalists**   **Reluctant conversationalists**

1. Share by the way you live, rather than by words
2. Ask questions about their beliefs and life experiences
3. Tell the other person about the changes and benefits of life in Christ
4. Spend time praying for the person and your time together before you get together
5. Tell them the story of how you first came to believe in Jesus
6. Quote passages from the Bible
7. Use the same basic approach every time you share your faith
8. Send something digitally
9. Challenge them to defend their lifestyle or beliefs in view of your beliefs and convictions

n = 796 U.S. self-identified Christians, June 22–July 13, 2017.

FIGURE 5.6

Paul says we are to use wisdom in figuring out "how [we] ought to answer each person." Rather than aggressively inserting a memorized gospel summary into a conversation, we are to graciously respond in a thoughtful way to the person we are talking to. This is a posture eager conversationalists appear to have learned.

Based on this biblical call to graciously adapt in conversations, Lutheran Hour Ministries has developed a simple tool for helping Christians begin to be thoughtful and wise about how they respond to the specific non-Christian they are talking to. The "Spiritual Conversation Curve" (fig. 5.7) is based on research in a variety of fields and lays out the basic spiritual postures non-Christians have toward the gospel in our age (unreceptive, receptive, or seeking). It indicates what kind of prayerful response is most fitting for each (gain a hearing, give good news, guide toward faith). The curve also breaks down the six conversation types that are useful in graciously adapting to where someone is in their journey.[2] This model is simply a way to help us develop the habit of gracious adaptation in conversations.

There is good reason for all of us to pause and reflect on our own conversational posture. The research indicates Christians are more likely than twenty-five years ago to use the same basic approach and content whenever they talk about their faith. Is it possible this tendency to rely on a single response is part of what accounts for our overall silence? Perhaps we know intuitively that it can be ungentle and disrespectful to insert memorized gospel-speak into a conversation.

By contrast, those who talk about their faith more (our eager conversationalists) are open to a variety of faith-sharing approaches. Having a habit of gracious adaptation makes it easier to talk about our faith. This is what Paul was getting at when he encouraged the Colossians to be wise and figure out how "to answer each person."

SPIRITUAL CONVERSATION CURVE

FROM LUTHERAN HOUR MINISTRIES

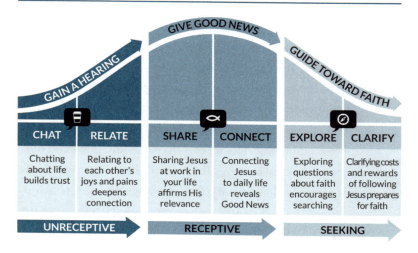

FIGURE 5.7

In reality there is nothing new about this posture of gracious adaptation. In a sense this is what Paul modeled for the church in his own ministry. In 1 Corinthians 9, Paul explains why he adapts his mode of sharing about Jesus based on who he is talking to:

> Though I am free from all, I have made myself a servant to all, that I might win more of them. To the Jews I became as a Jew, in order to win Jews. To those under the law I became as one under the law . . . that I might win those under the law. To those outside the law I became as one outside the law . . . that I might win those outside the law. To the weak I became weak, that I might win the weak. I have become all things to all people, that by all means I might save some. I do it all for the sake of the gospel, that I may share with them in its blessings. (1 Corinthians 9:19-23)

Just as Paul spoke one way while in a Jewish synagogue and another way while in a pagan marketplace, so we too today can graciously adapt our sharing based on the context. The overriding concern: that we might save more. This is undoubtedly part of what Peter was getting at when encouraging the Christians in Asia Minor to respond to non-Christians with "gentleness and respect." What is more gentle and respectful than taking someone's posture and journey seriously and responding to them as the person they are rather than quoting at them some memorized witness jargon? When we take someone seriously and respond to them, we can do it in "good conscience" as Peter encouraged.

> When faith comes up in a conversation, what do you tend to say or talk about?
>
> How do you discern where a non-Christian friend is in their spiritual journey?
>
> Consider a non-Christian in your life through the lens of the "Spiritual Conversation Curve." How does this simple model affect how you see or understand where your friend is on their journey? How does it help you discern how you could be most helpful to them?

Habit 4. Eager conversationalists gently push through the awkward moments. Peter was very clear in his letter to the Christians in Asia Minor that there were going to be tough times for Christians, but that this sober reality should not make them fearful or quiet: "Even if you should suffer for righteousness' sake, you will be blessed. Have no fear of them, nor be troubled, but in your hearts honor Christ the Lord as holy, always being prepared to make a defense to anyone who asks you for a reason for the hope that is in you" (1 Peter 3:14-15).

This is another conversational habit of eager conversationalists. As we explored earlier, they are just as likely to experience some tension or conflict in a conversation as reluctant conversationalists. However, they are simply faithful to not abandon ship when that happens. The research suggests they are not willing to be stopped by the tension or conflict but they gently press on in the conversation. This could be where their beliefs about the afterlife and the Christian's role as witness come into play: if hearing about Jesus is that important, it's worth pushing through the beginnings of potential conflict.

And as a result, eager conversationalists get to an enjoyable, positive place: they experience more joy, gladness, and peace in conversations. It turns out a little conflict isn't the end of the world, as we thought previously, and eager conversationalists are willing to stay in a conversation long enough to experience that firsthand. This is one of their conversational habits and could be one of yours and mine as well.

Beau Crosetto writes about this habit of pushing through the awkwardness in a spiritual conversation in his book *Beyond Awkward*, suggesting there are huge benefits that come from being willing to gently push through the awkward stage of a conversation. "Most of the time when God asks us to talk to someone in his name, it will be awkward at some point. But right after some of the initial tension is released, some kind of breakthrough comes, whether in the other person, in us or in the conversation."[3] Crosetto's book is, at its core, an invitation to embrace the habit eager conversationalists have: "You have to embrace awkwardness which is the gateway to many break-throughs with people around you."[4]

Back in that classroom I saw both sides of this coin. Because I was willing to push through the awkwardness of moment 1 (raising my hand to the rhetorical question) and moment 2 (sharing why I believed what I did), I was able to see something extraordinary: someone's walls coming down and their true feelings and tensions coming out.

But then moment 3 came (my professor's surprisingly vul-nerable confession), and I bailed out of the conversation. Perhaps this was due in part to the fraught nature of our situ-ation (he was a paid professor, and we were his graded students within a secular organization), perhaps it was my own fear. Who knows what I would have experienced had I pressed through that third awkward moment and stayed engaged in the blossoming spiritual conversation?

Describe a moment in a conversation when you sensed awkwardness or a potential conflict. What was your knee-jerk reaction? Has that always been your first reaction?

Describe a time when you pushed through potential conflict (with gentleness and respect) to get to the joy on the other side. What did that conversation teach you?

Exploring Four Simple Conversational Habits

Taken as a whole, these conversational habits give us a modern-day insight into what it would be like to take Peter's invitation in 1 Peter 3 seriously:

- to expect spiritual conversations (people are going to ask us about the hope within us)

- to pursue and initiate spiritual conversations (always being prepared to talk about our faith)

- to be responsive to the person we're talking with (treating them with gentleness and respect)

- to push through the awkward moments (not afraid or troubled by the gospel being out of season)

Notice Peter isn't inviting the Christians of Asia Minor to be perfect conversationalists. That's never an option. He's not asking them to convince everyone of the veracity of the gospel. That's not within our power. He *is* asking them to take on a certain posture—a fascinating mix of strength and humility: no fear, but plenty of gentleness; not perfect, but having a good conscience.

Did I handle that conversation back in college perfectly? Looking back, I would say I didn't. You know what they say about hindsight. But did I treat Professor Steve with gentleness and respect? I would say I did. Instead of striking back or pointing a finger at these morally loose classmates and professor, I gave a reason for the hope that was in me and did it while respecting them.

Maybe I didn't swim perfectly, but I was willing to jump into the waters of witness. Maybe I didn't say everything I could have, but I did walk through the open door that presented itself. And it turns out that matters. How much does our willingness matter? Let's return to those simple words Paul wrote to the Colossians: "Walk in wisdom toward outsiders, making the best use of the time. Let your speech always be gracious, seasoned with salt, so that you may know how you ought to answer each person" (Colossians 4:5-6).

Paul says that being wise in our interactions with non-Christians is "making the best use of the time." In the Greek language Paul was using to write to the Colossians, he had the choice of two words for "time" in this verse: *chronos* and *kairos*. The first word, *chronos*, refers to the simple passage of time—"ticktock" time if you will. The second word, *kairos*, refers to a pregnant moment of time—"the time has come" time if you will. Paul uses the second word. Make the most use of the *moments* you find yourself in.

When God opens doors in conversations for us, do we make the most use of those moments? Do we "cash in" on those moments? (That's how Paul's Greek literally reads.) Or do those moments pass us by, "uncashed in," if you will? These are haunting words from Paul to consider because they underscore the importance of our willingness to jump into the waters of witness.

Considering Paul's words makes me glad God, slowly over time, is helping me become a little less reluctant and a little more eager. Paul's words make me glad God's Word provides such sound guidance for how to lean in to spiritual conversations. His words make me appreciate the latest research and the example of all these eager conversationalists. Ultimately, this is why I'm glad you've come on this five-chapter journey with me.

My prayer is that we all develop some of these conversational habits for ourselves. May we begin to expect more spiritual conversations. May we begin to pursue and initiate some of those conversations. May we graciously adapt to the people we get into conversations with. May we have the grace and courage to push through the awkward moments.

May our feet become a little more beautiful over time.

Conclusion

Back on the Bus

So, I'm thirteen-and-a-half hours into my bus ride from the desert town of Ontario, Oregon, to the rainy town of Tacoma, Washington. And I haven't spoken a word to the woman seated next to me for the entire trip.

But I'm also three-fourths of the way through Becky Manley Pippert's book *Out of the Saltshaker and into the World*, where Pippert writes about spiritual conversations as if they are normal, beautiful, everyday things. As if they are the way God sometimes steps in and changes lives. As if being willing to enter into conversation somehow makes your feet beautiful.

And I'm starting to wonder, *Are the waters of witness really great?* So, after 13½ hours of riding in complete silence, I turned to the woman seated next to me and said (remember how brilliant my opening line was?), "Hi."

You've already read this part of the story. The woman seated next to me flinched just slightly and her eyes widened, she smiled politely, and said, "Hey."

And there we were, both of us, on the trailhead of a conversation. Taking that first step, I had no idea where that conversation would go or if it would go at all. Turns out it did. And it has become an unforgettable lesson for me about the true beauty and power of spiritual conversations.

A few years earlier a fellow who sat next to me on a plane had asked, politely, "Are you coming or going?" I thought it was a clever way of making polite small talk while in transit, and I had adopted it as my go-to line when I found myself in that awkward space of small talk while traveling. And so, sitting there on the bus, I went to my go-to line as a next tentative step in the conversation: "So, are you coming or going?"

I'm not sure if at the time I expected much more than a polite conversation about our respective itineraries. I do know I did not expect what happened next. The woman paused and looked down at her feet, as if in thought. Then she looked up at me and said, "I'm not really sure."

Walking up a trail is interesting. Each step takes you a little higher, which means two things. First, it takes some real effort, walking uphill is not easy. And second, the view changes with each step. It's amazing what new vistas, what hidden valleys open up to our sight the further up a trail we get. And that's exactly what happened on that bus. Just a couple steps up the trail, just a few exchanged words, brought us somewhere. *I'm not really sure?* How can someone not know if they are leaving home to go somewhere or coming back home from somewhere? I was confused and responded by saying, "Oh."

I know, brilliant repartee. An awkward step forward in the conversation. But that's all it took. God opened a door right then and there on that bus. Without further prompting, she began sharing her story. How she had gotten deep into an unhealthy cycle (lots of drugs) while living in Los Angeles and how her life was spiraling out of control. How she had moved to Las Vegas to get a fresh start and get away from all the unhealthy relationships and connections she had in the drug scene. How within her first week in Las Vegas she could already tell who at her new job was a supplier. "You can just tell," she told me. "Once you're in that lifestyle you can just tell who's using, who to ask to set you up."

Out spilled her story as we sat together on the bus, the miles clicking by. That first week in Vegas she had found a supplier, had started using again, had developed a new group of friends who all used. And just like that she was back in the same unhealthy cycle. She could feel her life slipping away.

But she wanted more. She didn't want to waste her life. She had a little bit of hope: her sister who lived in Seattle had invited her to move in with her. Get a fresh start in a new city, get cleaned up. Get some new friends. So, she had some hope, a little hope. But I'll never forget the mixture of hope and despair in her voice as she shared the war going on inside of her:

> I had such hopes for Vegas. I felt I'd really get to start over there, but there's also something in me that just wanted to get back into the lifestyle. I slipped back into it so easily. So, I'm a little hopeful for Seattle, for a fresh start like my sister says, but part of me worries I'll find a supplier within a week and be right back where I came from. I'm not sure if there really is any hope for me.

Let me pause the conversation at this point. Reflecting back, I am so struck by how little it took from me to spark this conversation. Three short lines: *Hi. Are you coming or going? Oh.* That's it. Three simple steps forward: just putting one foot in front of the other. And just three short steps up the trailhead of this conversation and we were having a spiritual conversation about life, temptation, hope.

I'm also struck by how natural and beautiful this conversation was. Remember, I had been laboring under the illusion spiritual conversations were pesky, painful, awkward things. But this was anything but. It was real. It was important. It was beautiful to see her sharing her burdens and hopes and temptations with someone else. To not be so alone. It was just like Becky Pippert had written. It was just like Paul had said, just like Isaiah had described it—it was beautiful.

I'm not sure if there really is any hope for me. Our conversation had brought us to this tender place of honesty and desperation inside of her. And so, I, in faltering words, spilled my own story out into the bus between us. I told her about my own unhealthy cycles, my own temptations. And then I told her of a place (a kingdom, not another city) where I had found hope. I shared the ways being in God's kingdom had started healthy cycles in my life, how I was beginning to heal. How hope had become real and solid in my life.

For an hour and a half we spoke of sin and temptation and hope and healing and reconciliation. And she held the gospel message in her hands tentatively, considering it for the first time in her life. Daring to believe that maybe there really was hope for her after all.

> How beautiful upon the mountains
>> are the feet of him who brings good news,
> who publishes peace, who brings good news of
>>> happiness,
> who publishes salvation. (Isaiah 52:7)

It was true, I realized. There is something beautiful about our readiness to bring good news. There is something delightful about spiritual conversations. What I experienced on that bus ride is proclaimed in Scripture and, as we have seen, confirmed by the latest research. These eager conversationalists really have tapped into something delightful. The water really is great—it's warm and refreshing and, yes, even enjoyable.

And aside from how delightful it turns out spiritual conversations can be, it almost goes without saying how important they are. People need good news. They need peace. They become desperate for happiness, for salvation, for hope. And they are sitting right next to us.

We can't make a spiritual conversation happen. But as I found out that day on that bus ride, we can take a couple of steps, one foot in front of the other, onto the trailhead of a conversation. You never know where it might go.

I may have waited 13½ hours before starting that conversation, but the last hour and a half of the ride were unforgettable because I simply turned and said hi. In hindsight, I've become so grateful that we stopped at *every single little town* on the way. Every bus station we pulled into, every slowdown in traffic I see now as blessed extensions of our important conversation.

But eventually the bus ride had to come to an end. After an hour and a half we were pulling into Tacoma. This would be my stop. She would continue north to Seattle and her new life. We were sharing my sack lunch (she didn't have any food or much money with her), and we both realized our conversation was about to come to an end. We had gone deep, had shared vulnerably, had talked about the kingdom of God and the good news of hope. I remember I was eating a green apple as we turned off the highway and started making our way through city streets to the bus terminal in downtown Tacoma.

As my stop got closer we realized we had never even introduced ourselves. We had climbed together up the heights of a deep conversation learning each other's temptations and hopes but didn't even know each other's name. So, we told each other our names and then I asked, innocently enough, "So, what do you do?"

She looked surprised by the question. And answered, tentatively, "Oh, I'm a dancer." That sounded like an interesting job. So, I asked, "Oh, like ballet?" She smiled sheepishly at this. "No, more like exotic dancing." She looked embarrassed, but I still didn't catch on (this is an embarrassing but unfortunately true part of the story) and asked, naively, "Oh, like folk dancing?"

She smiled and shrugged and then said, her voice going up as if in question, "No, more like . . . lap dancing?" And my eyes got wide. I finally got it. The tumblers falling into place. And then she asked me, "So, what do you do?"

And now it was my turn to look surprised by the question. I answered, vaguely, "Oh, I work at a university." She looked impressed. "Like a professor?" I smiled sheepishly. "No, I do mentoring work, helping students grow." She looked a little confused and asked, "So . . . like a coach?"

And I smiled and shrugged and then said, my voice going up as if in question, "No, more like . . . a pastor?"

And her eyes got wide. And there we sat—the stripper and the campus pastor—our eyes wide. And then we burst out laughing at the unlikelihood of our conversation, the improbability of our shared vulnerability. We laughed and laughed, so much so that I saw tears streaming down her face as the bus turned right into the bus terminal in downtown Tacoma. And that was the end of our conversation.

Reflecting back, I wonder if some of those tears making their way down her face were not from the laughter but from having been offered good news. Tears coming from daring to believe that perhaps there was hope for her after all. I wonder what happened when she got to Seattle. I wonder what she did with that good news she held in her hands for the first time. I wonder what Christian God sent into her life in Seattle to talk with her next. I wonder if she is somewhere today telling this same story and marveling at the delight of spiritual conversations.

Thinking back to that bus ride gives me hope. I hope God continues to make my feet more and more beautiful as time goes by. I hope God helps the church find its voice again. I hope God's word helps us become wiser, more gracious, gentler, and more eager in our conversations with the people sitting right next to us in life.

I hope we turn and say hi more often. I hope we step onto the trailheads of conversations more often. I hope God gives us the courage and humility to simply put one foot in front of the other and see what happens. I hope he uses our inelegant, imperfect efforts to do something elegant and perfect in the lives of the people sitting right next to us.

Why use silly people like you and me to bring good news to others? Why not use impressive and rhetorically brilliant evangelists? Perhaps it's because when God uses folks like us it brings glory to him. As Paul made so clear, "We have this treasure in jars of clay, to show that the surpassing power belongs to God and not to us" (2 Corinthians 4:7).

Okay, so you are a humble clay pot. You tend toward reluctance. All right. You are exactly the kind of person God wants to use.

The good news is that anyone who calls on the name of the Lord will be saved. But how will they call on someone they don't believe in? And how will they believe in someone they've never heard about? And how will they hear unless someone tells them about him?

And what if God wants that person to be you?

Acknowledgments

AFTER GETTING TO KNOW ME in the preceding pages, I imagine you might be thinking, *There must have been so many kind, helpful, and patient friends, leaders, and ministries to get Don from the safe banks of reluctance into the delightful waters of witness.* You would be right.

Writing this book has only refreshed and strengthened my gratitude for the beloved brothers and sisters who have walked alongside me through my journey—especially those in the two wonderful kingdom tribes known as InterVarsity Christian Fellowship and the Covenant Order of Evangelical Presbyterians.

It was my privilege to write this book as a glad member of a new, robust partnership (and virtual think tank) between Lutheran Hour Ministries and Barna Group. Special thanks to Tony Cook and David Kinnaman for inviting me to the table, and to Jason Broge for helping me through both the tedious and rapturous moments of writing this book.

Finally, my conversation partners: Though I have changed your names for this book, you know who you are. You know just how grateful I am for your friendship. And, perhaps more than any other readers, you know exactly how "clay" I am and therefore how "surpassing" God's power must be.

Appendix 1

Research Partners

Barna Group

Barna Group (barna.com) is a research firm dedicated to providing actionable insights on faith and culture, with a particular focus on the Christian church. In its thirty-year history, Barna has conducted more than one million interviews in the course of hundreds of studies and has become a go-to source for organizations that want to better understand a complex and changing world from a faith perspective.

Lutheran Hour Ministries

Lutheran Hour Ministries (lhm.org) is a trusted resource in global media that equips and engages a vibrant volunteer base to passionately proclaim the gospel to more than 125 million people worldwide each week. Through its North American headquarters and thirty-four ministry centers on six continents, LHM reaches into more than fifty countries, often bringing Christ to places where no other Christian evangelistic organizations are present.

LHM and Barna are partnering together on a three-year research endeavor to reveal how Americans are expressing their faith. *The Reluctant Witness* is based on the first year of research, which looks at how individuals engage in spiritual conversations. The second year of research will focus on the influence of households on spiritual development, and the third year will look at the impact of Christians on the broader community. Don Everts will be working with InterVarsity Press to produce a book based on each year of research.

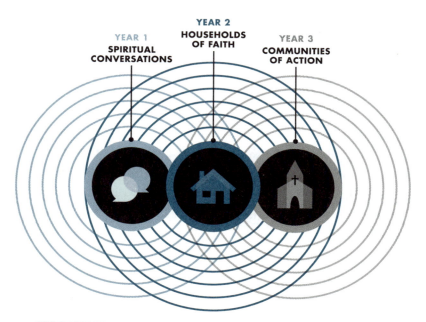

Appendix 2

Research Methodology

In-Depth Survey (Qualitative)

An exploratory, open-ended, online survey was conducted among 102 Christians to understand more about their spiritual conversations as well as online interactions. This survey was conducted between April 20 and May 15, 2017.

Nationally Representative Survey (Quantitative)

The primary source of data in this report is a survey of 1,714 US adults, composed of an oversample of 535 millennials and 689 practicing Christians, conducted online from June 22 to July 13, 2017. Respondents were recruited from a national consumer panel, and minimal weighting was applied to ensure representation of certain demographic factors, such as age, gender, ethnicity, and region. The sample error for this data is plus or minus 2.2 percent at the 95 percent confidence level for the total sample. A subgroup of participants had either "shared my views on faith or religion in the last 5 years" or "someone has shared their views on faith or religion with me in the last 5 years."[1]

Appendix 3

Definitions

The following definitions are from "Spiritual Conversations in the Digital Age."[1]

Self-identified Christians select "Christian" from a list of religious affiliations.

Non-Christians do not self-identify as Christian.

Churched Christians identify as Christian and have attended church within the past six months.

Unchurched Christians identify as Christian but have not attended church within the past six months.

Practicing Christians identify as Christian, have attended church within the past month, and strongly agree that their faith is very important in their life today.

Nonpracticing Christians identify as Christian but do not qualify as practicing under the definition above.

Eager conversationalists identify as Christian and have had ten or more conversations about faith in the past year.

Reluctant conversationalists identify as Christian and have had between zero and nine conversations about faith in the past year.

Gen Z were born from 1999 to 2015 (only 13- to 18-year-olds included).

Millennials were born from 1984 to 1998.

Gen X were born from 1965 to 1983.

Boomers were born from 1946 to 1964.

Elders were born before 1946.

Notes

Introduction

[1]Rebecca Manley Pippert, *Out of the Saltshaker and into the World: Evangelism as a Way of Life*, 2nd ed. (Downers Grove, IL: InterVarsity Press, 1999).

[2]For more information see appendix 1: "Research Partners."

Chapter 1: Reluctant Conversationalists

[1]For more information on how this research was conducted see appendix 2: "Research Methodology."

[2]Barna Group, "Spiritual Conversations in the Digital Age: How Christians' Approach to Sharing Their Faith Has Changed in 25 Years" (Ventura, CA: Barna Group, 2018).

[3]For a list of generations (and accompanying birth years) see appendix 3: "Definitions."

[4]For more information see John Suler, "The Online Disinhibition Effect," *CyberPsychology and Behavior* 7, no. 3 (July 2004): 321-26.

[5]Check out the booklet by Rachel Legouté and Don Everts, *My Digital Voice: An Introduction to the Digital Conversation Pledge* at www.lhm.org/projectconnect.

Chapter 2: Why We Stopped Talking

[1]David Kinnaman and Gabe Lyons, *Good Faith: Being a Christian When Society Thinks You're Irrelevant and Extreme* (Grand Rapids: Baker, 2016).

Chapter 3: Delightful Conversations

[1]Barna Group, "Spiritual Conversations in the Digital Age: How Christians' Approach to Sharing Their Faith Has Changed in 25 Years" (Ventura, CA: Barna Group, 2018), 49.

[2]Interestingly, the numbers are a bit higher when laying the blame of stirring up conflict on your conversation partner. The same dynamic is in place relative to respect: it's more common to perceive that you were not respected than to admit you did not respect the other. Perhaps we are quicker to lay the blame at someone else's feet than at our own?

Chapter 4: Eager Conversationalists

[1]The only demographic difference that popped up was having children—being a parent seems to correlate to having more faith conversations. Twenty-nine percent of Christians with children are eager conversationalists whereas only 21 percent of those without children are eager conversationalists.

[2]For more information see James Choung, *True Story: A Christianity Worth Believing In* (Downers Grove, IL: InterVarsity Press, 2008), or watch James Choung present the diagram at "The Big Story, Part 1," *YouTube*, September 11, 2007, https://youtu.be/kCVcSiUUMhY.

[3]"Prepared to Respond: Exploring the Spiritual Conversation Curve," Lutheran Hour Ministries, 2018, can be found at www.lhm.org /learn/outreach-essentials.

[4]For more information see Don Everts and Doug Schaupp, *I Once Was Lost: What Postmodern Skeptics Taught Us About Their Path to Jesus* (Downers Grove, IL: InterVarsity Press, 2008).

Chapter 5: Everyday Conversations

[1]Don Everts, Val Gordon, and Doug Schaupp, *Breaking the Huddle: How Your Community Can Grow Its Witness* (Downers Grove, IL: InterVarsity Press, 2016).

[2]For more information on the Spiritual Conversation Curve go to www.lhm.org/curve to find an introductory booklet, a free online course, and pocket-sized Curve Cards.

[3]Beau Crosetto, *Beyond Awkward: When Talking About Jesus Is Outside Your Comfort Zone* (Downers Grove, IL: InterVarsity Press, 2014), 42.

[4]Crosetto, *Beyond Awkward*, 16.

Appendix 2

[1]Barna Group, "Spiritual Conversations in the Digital Age: How Christians' Approach to Sharing Their Faith Has Changed in 25 Years" (Ventura, CA: Barna Group, 2018), 91.

Appendix 3

[1]Barna Group, "Spiritual Conversations in the Digital Age: How Christians' Approach to Sharing Their Faith Has Changed in 25 Years" (Ventura, CA: Barna Group, 2018), 92.

About the Author

REVEREND DON EVERTS has worked as an ordained pastor in the local church for over a decade, and before that worked for fourteen years on college campuses with InterVarsity Christian Fellowship. Whether in the church or on campus, Don has walked with folks who are not Christian as they discover the person of Jesus, and he has worked with Christians in being able to fruitfully do the same in their own relationships. An award-winning author, he has written books for seekers and skeptics (including *Jesus with Dirty Feet*) and for Christians who want to grow in their personal witness (including *I Once Was Lost, Go and Do*, and *Breaking the Huddle*).

Don currently works with a team of writers, thinkers, educators, and leaders at Lutheran Hour Ministries to create cutting-edge, research-based, biblical resources that help equip Christians and churches everywhere to spread the good news in winsome, fruitful ways. More information on these resources can be found at www.lhm.org.

Don and his wife, Wendy, have three children and live in the St. Louis area.

Other Titles by Don Everts

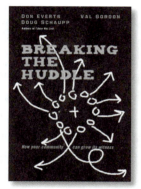

Breaking the Huddle
978-0-8308-4491-3

I Once Was Lost
978-0-8308-3608-6

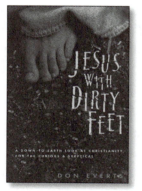

Jesus with Dirty Feet
978-0-8308-2206-5

Go and Do
978-0-8308-3822-6